Elizabethan Treasures

Elizabethan Treasures
The Hardwick Hall Textiles

SANTINA M. LEVEY

THE NATIONAL TRUST

Distributed by
Harry N. Abrams, Inc., Publishers

First published in Great Britain in 1998 by
National Trust Enterprises Ltd
36 Queen Anne's Gate, London SW1H 9AS

Reprinted 1999

Distributed in North America in 1988 by
Harry N. Abrams, Incorporated, New York

Library of Congress Catalog Card Number:
98-70062

ISBN 0-8109-6353-1

 Harry N. Abrams, Inc.
100 Fifth Avenue
New York, N.Y. 10011
www.abramsbooks.com

Designed by the Newton Engert Partnership

Production by Dee Maple

Phototypeset in Monotype Garamond 156 by
SPAN Graphics, Crawley, West Sussex

Printed and bound in Great Britain by
Butler & Tanner Ltd

1 (*half title*) Fragment of unfaded embroidery
*c.*1570. Cut-pile velvet with applied motifs cut
from red and green cloths of gold and silver and
embroidered with silver and silver-gilt purl, gold
and silver thread, and cord couched with coloured
silks, partly over padding. (Detail: 16 × 12cm)
Inv. T/366 *SML*

2 (*frontispiece*) The warrior queen, Zenobia,
from one of the large appliqué hangings *c.*1573.
Her clothes and the architectural setting are cut
from rich fabrics salvaged from ecclesiastical
vestments, including cut-velvets, patterned
cloths of gold, and multi-coloured silk damasks,
with details embroidered with metal threads,
partly over padding, and applied silk and metal
bobbin lace. (Height of figure 116cm) Inv. T/231c
NTPL/John Hammond

The author and the publisher would like to thank the following
for permission to reproduce the plates listed below:

(**6**) The Stedelijke Musea, Courtrai, Belgium.

(**8**) Courtauld Institute of Art.

(**9**), (**76** photograph: Courtauld Institute of Art), (**80**), (**84**), (**90**), (**95**)
Devonshire Collection, Chatsworth. Reproduced by permission of the
Duke of Devonshire and the Chatsworth Settlement Trustees.

(**21**) By kind permission of His Grace the Duke of Buccleuch and
Queensberry, K.T., from his collection at Boughton House,
Northamptonshire.

(**43**) Courtesy of the British Library.

(**32**), (**45**), (**50**), (**53**), (**74**) Courtesy of the Victoria & Albert Museum
Picture Library (*V&A*).

(**71**) Courtesy of Anthony Wells-Cole.

(**31**), (**72**), (**87**) Copyright holders not known, although every effort has
been made to trace them.

All other illustrations are the property of the author (*SML*), the National
Trust (*NT*), or the National Trust Photographic Library (*NTPL*)

Author's Acknowledgements
This book could not have been written without the generosity of the
late John L. Nevinson, who introduced me to the Hardwick textiles and
who made provision in his will for the completion of his work on them.
In following in his footsteps, I have drawn not only on his work but on
that of many others, in particular of David Durant and Mark Girouard.
I am very grateful to them for their encouragement and willingness to
answer my questions, and also to Nicolas Barker and John Cornforth who
have been similarly kind in providing practical advice and help. One of the
major pleasures has been the exchange of ideas and information with other
specialists – every one of them an enthusiast – and I offer my warmest
thanks to Janet Arnold, Rosemary Crill, Wendy Hefford, David Mitchell,
Lisa Monnas, Natalie Rothstein, Jennifer Wearden and Anthony Wells-Cole;
this would have been a poorer book without their contributions.

The most important research material has been the textiles themselves,
and for making them accessible I have to thank the Administrator at
Hardwick, Christopher Corry-Thomas, and all the house staff, who have
been unfailingly kind in satisfying my demands for ladders, lights and
'another pair of hands'. Nettie Cook and John Entwhistle gave me much
practical help and, above all, I am grateful to the Curator, Gillian White,
for her unfailing support – far beyond the call of duty – and always
given with tolerant good humour. I was equally fortunate at Chatsworth,
where Peter Day, the Keeper of the Collections, always provided a warm
welcome and practical help when I needed access to the Archive. Some
of the textiles are temporarily in store at the Victoria and Albert Museum,
and I have to thank my former colleagues in the Department of Textiles
for allowing me constant access, and Clare Browne in particular for her
quiet and unfailing support. Many of the National Trust's staff, both in
the Regions and at Head Quarters, have helped with the book, but I am
especially grateful to Ksynia Marko for her comments on the Tobit table
carpet, which she is conserving, and for providing photographs. Above all
I have to thank Helen Fewster for overseeing the publication of the book
with all that entails, not least a tender concern for the sensibilities of the
author. Finally, I am grateful to Miklós Rajnai for his wise advice and
willingness to listen.

CONTENTS

INTRODUCTION

This book is about the textile furnishings at Hardwick Hall in Derbyshire and in particular about those that belonged to the Dowager Countess of Shrewsbury, the redoubtable Bess of Hardwick. Their importance is best expressed in her own words as set out in her will of April 1601:

> yt hath pleased god to give me leave to undertake and performe some buildinges at my houses at Chatesworthe, hardwicke and oldcoates … and to obtayne some plate bedding hangings and other furniture of household stuffe the which I greatlie desire should be well preserved and contynuede at my said houses for the better furnishing thereof.

This is repeated three times as she deals with each of the houses and she also stipulates that none of the 'said plate bedding hangings and other furniture of household stuffe' may be disposed of by 'will, gifte or other devise to any other person or persons', and, finally, she instructs her heirs to:

> have speciall care and regard to p'serve the same from all manner of wett, mothe and other hurte or spoyle therofe and to leave them so preserved to contynewe at the sayed several houses as a foresayed for the better furnishyng them therewithall.[1]

Bess of Hardwick lived at a time when textiles were of prime importance; they were the major means of providing colour, pattern, warmth and comfort within a house, and their high cost made them the vehicle for an often ostentatious display of wealth. It has been calculated, for example, that the New Hall at Hardwick cost about £5,000–£6,000 to build, admittedly using raw materials mainly from Bess's own estates, but the textile furnishings were worth considerably more and, despite the fact that relatively few of them were new, they were still highly valued.[2] They included, for example, a bed with pearl-embroidered furnishings made for Bess and her second husband Sir William Cavendish in 1547 which was still of sufficient importance in 1607 to be the subject of a codicil to her will (see p.39).

In the sixteenth century not even the wealthiest people equipped their several houses to the same degree of comfort; the Queen always travelled accompanied by her Removing Wardrobe of furnishings and clothes, and great landowners similarly transferred their textile goods from one house to another as need arose. For as long as Hardwick was one of a number of family houses, its contents were liable to be moved and, as we shall see, such moves could lead to disputes over ownership. Attitudes towards textiles, in particular to the quantity in which they were used and their importance relative to other forms of wall covering and upholstery, were, however, to change from the late seventeenth century onwards. From that time also, with the rebuilding of Chatsworth by the 1st Duke of Devonshire, Hardwick became less important. It never ceased to be used by the family, however, and never became the sort of 'sleeping-beauty' palace that has sometimes been imagined. Although in the eighteenth century conscious efforts began to be made to preserve the oldest furnishings, changes continued not only until the house was handed over to the National Trust in 1959 but beyond.

The textiles now in the house cannot therefore be used to re-create its interior as it was at any particular period but what they can do is bring alive the people who have lived there over the centuries and, above all, provide a direct and very personal link to Bess herself. For, despite the depredations of time, Hardwick contains the most important collection of original sixteenth-century furnishings in any house in England, and Bess was intimately involved with their acquisition. Particularly important to her were the embroideries and pieces of needlework, many of which were made within her household; they include some unique items and, in their quality and quantity, outweigh in importance the other surviving textiles. Consequently, they will form the subject of a catalogue to be published as a second volume where full technical descriptions and information about the sources of their designs and subject-matter will be provided. They will also be assessed in relation to other surviving pieces and to relevant descriptions in sixteenth-century archival material. Here, however, they will be considered, together with the other textiles, in the context of Bess's life and the lives of her descendants. The processes of buying or making the various furnishings will be examined, as well as the changes in styles of living and interior design that dictated the steady alteration of the house.

3 Detail of the *Fancie of a Fowler* cushion (fig. **57**) showing the rich effects achieved by combining different threads and stitches. Inv. T/152 *NTPL/John Hammond*

MARIA REGINA

Chapter One

BEFORE THE BUILDING
OF THE NEW HALL

In 1590, when the Countess of Shrewsbury embarked on the building of her New Hall at Hardwick, she drew upon the knowledge and experience of a long and eventful life and, from a mixture of ideas and influences, she produced a masterpiece. Her earlier life was reflected even more directly by the furnishings with which the new house was filled, since many of them had been accumulated over the years and were important to her for their monetary value, for the statements they made about style and status, as well as for their personal associations.

The story of the Hardwick textiles therefore starts not in the 1590s but in 1547, with the marriage of the young widow Elizabeth Barley to the middle-aged Sir William Cavendish.[1] The marriage took place at Bradgate House in Leicestershire, the home of Lord Grey, Marquess of Dorset and his wife Frances, the daughter of Henry VIII's sister Mary Tudor. Bess was one of Lady Grey's gentlewomen and it was in her company that she attended the Court of Henry VIII, which, even in the King's declining years, was one of great splendour. The luxurious tapestries and embroidered furnishings apparently provided a yardstick for magnificence that stayed with Bess throughout her life.

William Cavendish (5) was a younger son who had benefited from the mobile economic and social climate of the day; through service at Court he had not only risen to be Treasurer of the King's Privy Purse and a Privy Councillor, but had acquired a knighthood, land and property, including the former monastic manor of Northaw in Hertfordshire. Following his marriage to Bess, however, he sold or exchanged his lands in the south for land in her native county of Derbyshire; the first purchase, in December 1549, included the manor of Chatsworth, and work on a house there began in 1551. Northaw was sold the following year. There is no doubt that Bess played a major part in this; indeed, given her later activities, it is probable that she initiated the whole venture. Since she had twice suffered the trauma of family estates being transferred to the Court of Wards, after the deaths of her father and the father of her first young husband, it is not surprising that the new house and lands were registered in the names of both Bess and her second husband. This was to protect the interests of their children should Sir William die before the eldest son came of age – as indeed happened.

Two of Sir William's daughters from his earlier marriages lived with them, and this ready-made family expanded rapidly as, between 1548 and 1557, eight more children were born, two of whom, Temperance and Lucretia, died in infancy. Members of Bess's own family often formed part of her household; early in her marriage, her half-sister and lifelong friend Jane Leche (later the wife of Thomas Kniveton), was one of her gentlewomen, with a quarterly salary of fifteen shillings,[2] and her aunt Marcella Linaker often held the fort at Northaw and later at Chatsworth when Bess was with her husband in London. On 14 November 1552, for example, Bess wrote instructing Francis Whitfield, the steward, to 'look well to all things at Chatsworth till my aunt's coming home, which I hope shall be shortly'. She was not pleased, however, with his behaviour towards Jane

4 (*left*) Bess as Lady Cavendish, painted by a follower of Eworth *c*.1557. She wears a quantity of jewellery and her fine clothes include a linen smock worked with red silk. The purchase of embroidery silk to decorate the Cavendishs' linen is recorded in an account book of 1548–50. *NTPL/Angelo Hornak*

5 (*below*) Sir William Cavendish, aged 44, painted by an unknown artist *c*.1550. He was Bess's second husband and the father of her children. Together they laid the foundations of the Cavendish (later Devonshire) estates and, although Sir William died in 1557, their marriage had a lasting impact on Bess's life. *NTPL*

6 Detail of a mid-16th-century linen damask table napkin from Flanders, woven with scenes of the *Sacrifice of Isaac* from the *Story of Abraham*. It was table linen of this type that Sir William Cavendish and Bess purchased in 1552. *Stedelijk Musea, Courtrai Inv. D.2064 (1986)*

Leche: 'I cannot like it to have my sister so used. Like as I would not have any superfluity or waste of anything, so likewise would I have her to have that which is needful and necessary.'[3] This is a neat summing-up of the manner in which she was to run her households throughout her life, and is also evident in the way she eventually furnished her New Hall at Hardwick.

Cavendish and Bess moved house in London not long after their marriage and, with the sale of Northaw and the rapid development of Chatsworth, Bess must have spent a lot of time planning and supervising the packing and installation of furniture and furnishings. In 1553 an inventory was taken of the more important objects at Chatsworth, and Bess checked, as well as signed, the two copies that were attached to a deed of entail 'to continue the same in the family'.[4] They were concerned solely with objects of lasting value, including thirty-six entries relating to gold and silver plate. Perhaps more difficult to appreciate today is the dominating presence of the textiles. Of these, the obviously most lasting were the forty-eight tapestries, some with silk highlights and others of 'coarser sort', and the two huge Turkish carpets measuring 21 and 15 feet long respectively. At that time such expensive imported goods were normally displayed on pieces of furniture, as in the case of the three smaller Turkish carpets 'for square bords' (tables) and twenty-one for cupboards – then decorative pieces of furniture similar to an open buffet with two or more shelves on which carpets and other covers were laid.

Listed before the carpets were fourteen fine beds, including one of 'gilte carv'd worke wth Sr Willm Cavendyshes and my ladye' armes', which was hung with vallances of red woollen cloth trimmed with red and silver braid. In general, however, the woodwork was much less important than the hangings. Those on Sir William's and Bess's marriage bed, for example, had 'doble valens of blacke velvytt ymbos'd wth clothe of golde and clothe of silu' {ye velvet} ymbrodered wth golde and perle wth v curtens of yelowe and white damaske, one cov'ing for the same bedd of blacke velvytt worc'd wth silu' ymbrodered with perle and purle, one very fine bedstead agreeable to the same bed, twoo chaires, one litle stole [stool] and one long cusshion of the same.' It was rare at that time for furnishings to be *en suite*, but almost all the other beds similarly had matching chairs, stools and cushions in a variety of materials: black and white velvet, cloth of silver and purple cloth of gold, white and tawny damask, red cloth embroidered with gold letters, murrey and yellow velvet cut quarter-wise and embroidered with gold and silver and trimmed with gold bobbin lace. The fine red woollen cloth may have been English, but all the silks and metal threads were imported, mainly via Antwerp, from Italy, Spain and the Near East, while from Flanders came the fine linen that completed the list of textiles. This included ten dozen napkins, ten long and ten square table cloths, all of damask, as well as six dozen pillowberes (pillow covers) and ten pairs of sheets of fine plain linen, and fifty pairs of sheets of coarser linen.

If any of these furnishings had been acquired specifically for Chatsworth, there is, with one exception, no record of their purchase, despite the existence of a series of account books covering the London house, Northaw, Chatsworth and, eventually, Hardwick.[5] Not only is the sequence of books incomplete but many entries simply note the total of a bill, as in a book of 1548–50, where payments of £8 and £10 were made to a mercer called Ledington – 'as by a byll appeareth'. What fabric he supplied and for what purpose is not known but the book does provide information about the cost of linen, huge quantities of which were needed to service a large household. This, together with the constant need to replenish the stock, meant that considerable sums of money were invested in it. The cost of linen was to feature later in the quarrel between Bess and her fourth husband, the Earl of Shrewsbury. Meanwhile, Bess noted the purchase of:

clothe that I boughte to make a paire of shetes after iij[s] iiij[d] a nell and yn the all xviij elnes	lij[s]
xij ellnes of clothe to make peloberes [pillow covers] after ij[s] the eln	xxiiij[s]
for clothe to make peloberes after xvj pence the elne for xij elnes	xvi[s6]

The differences in price reflected the quality of the linen, which in turn reflected the status of the users or the circumstances of its use. Thus Bess noted in the same book the purchase of a 'quarteren of fyne thread to sewe the lynen that was made agenste my Ladye Waryck comynge iij[s] iiij[d]'. Coarse sewing thread bought at the same time cost a shilling less per quarter pound. Many years later, in April 1586, after Mary Queen of Scots had been removed from Lord Shrewsbury's charge and taken to Chartley, Sir Amias Paulet wrote to Sir Francis Walsingham: 'It may please you to order that the linen for the Queen may be sent here, for her Majesty [Elizabeth] is the loser, because she [Mary] uses her best linen of damask every day.'[7]

The quantity of linen damask at Chatsworth in 1553 indicates the lavish style in which Cavendish and Bess lived. Its high cost, compared to that of the plain linens given above, is recorded in an entry, made on 14 November 1551, which may relate to some of the linen in the 1553 inventory (**6**):

paid for vj yards of fyne dyaper for one table clothe with the story of Abraham at xij[s] the yard	lxxij[s]

The matching napkins cost 2s 6d each, and the yardage linen for matching towels (for use at table) cost 4s a yard. In all, the set cost £9 16s at a time when Cavendish paid his butler 10s a quarter, and the higher servants 20s, that is £2 and £4 a year, to which were added board and lodging as well as a livery.[8]

Bess's marriage to William Cavendish was to have a lasting effect on her life. It produced the children to whose interests she was to devote so much of her energy, it laid

7 Sir William St Loe, Captain of the Guard to Queen Elizabeth I and Chief Butler of England. He married Bess as her third husband in 1559 and he died in 1564/5. Recent research has, however, cast doubt on this attribution. *NTPL*

the foundations of her estates, it saw the beginning of her first building venture and it established her within a network of important families, key members of which acted as godparents to her and Cavendish's children. They included the Greys; John Dudley, Earl of Warwick (later Duke of Northumberland) and his wife (their son, Robert Dudley, later Earl of Leicester, was also to be a close friend of Bess); Francis Talbot, 5th Earl of Shrewsbury and father of Bess's fourth husband; Elizabeth Brooke, daughter of Lord Cobham and wife of William Parr, Marquess of Northampton (she was to become the sister-in-law both of Cavendish's eldest daughter Catherine and of William Herbert, 2nd Earl of Pembroke). William Herbert was one of the godfathers to Bess and Cavendish's second son William (b.1551) and his grandson was to marry Bess's granddaughter, Mary Talbot. These people were supporters of the then Princess Elizabeth, who was godmother to Henry (b.1550), Bess and Cavendish's eldest son. Diplomatically, the Catholic Queen Mary was invited to be godmother to their third boy Charles (b.1553), whose second godfather, Stephen Gardner, Bishop of Winchester, was also a political choice, as William Paulet, the Lord Treasurer, had been for William.

The age difference between Sir William and Bess meant that she bridged two generations of this group, which was linked by its members' Protestant sympathies, intermarriages and cultural interests. During the ten-year span of the marriage, Bess formed lasting friendships and no doubt absorbed a great deal of literary and artistic knowledge on which she was to build during the remainder of her life.

Sir William Cavendish died after a short illness on 25 October 1557, leaving Bess not only with a large family of young children but also with an unexplained sum, in excess of £5,000, missing from the Privy Purse Account, for which he had been responsible and for which she was now liable. It is not surprising that she saw remarriage as one way of securing her and her children's financial future. On 15 August 1559 she married Sir William St Loe, Captain of the Queen's Guard, whom Elizabeth had that year made Chief Butler of England. This was a ceremonial role that kept Sir William tied to the Court, while Bess spent much time at Chatsworth.

Sir William St Loe (7) was a generous and supportive husband; in 1563 he paid £1,000 towards clearing Cavendish's debt to the crown and he seems actively to have encouraged his wife in her building work at Chatsworth. He helped with the dispatch of various goods from London and was also involved in settling her two elder sons, Henry and William Cavendish, at Eton College, together with all their 'Chamber Stuff', which had to be transported from London, complete with tenter hooks for the hangings.[9]

A second inventory of Chatsworth was apparently made at this time, although only a few rough notes survive.[10] None the less, they add a little to the information contained in the 1553 inventory. Several sets of tapestry are named, including four pieces 'off the story of Prodygus' (the *Prodigal Son*), seven of *David and Bathsheba* and four of *Solomon*. In addition, in Tymme's Chamber, there were 'ij of Davyd, one of Salom' Jugment, one of 'lle Raveshment, one off burning off hys hand'. Although this sounds like a mix of different sets, the survival at Hardwick of three pieces – the *Judgement of Solomon*, the *Rape of the Sabine Women* and the *Story of David* – all with matching borders, plus another of Mucius Scaevola thrusting his hand into the fire, and a fifth possibly showing King David, which have near-identical borders, suggests that this was a put-together set of heroes and that it has survived complete, if not undamaged.[11]

Bess was still sleeping in the 'bedde off red cloth trymd wth silu' lase' that she had shared with William Cavendish, whose portrait hung on the wall with one of William St Loe. The bed now had five curtains of red mockado, which ended up at Hardwick, while the great pearl bed was in the Noblemen's Chamber, reserved for visiting nobility.

The gentlemanly St Loe died in the winter of 1564–5 and Bess returned to Court as a Lady of the Privy Chamber, where she shared her duties with her lifelong friends Lady Stafford, Blanche Parry and Lady Cobham, who were later to keep her well informed about Court news. Among those moving in the same circles was George Talbot (**8**), who had become 6th Earl of Shrewsbury in 1560. His wife died in 1566, leaving him with seven children, of whom the two youngest boys were only 4 and 2 years old. Shrewsbury and Bess were both aged about 40, they had known one another socially for many years, and Sheffield Castle and Chatsworth House were only some 12 miles apart. It is not surprising that they both saw marriage as a solution to the practical difficulties of their situations.

In accordance with the practice of securing land and wealth by judicious marriages, an agreement was drawn up in January 1567/8 by which Lord Shrewsbury's eldest un-married son Gilbert was to marry Bess's daughter Mary, and her eldest son Henry was to marry Shrewsbury's daughter Grace.[12]

The marriage of Bess and Shrewsbury took place in the early autumn of 1567 and was to last for 23 years; it certainly started happily. Bess left the Court to live with her new husband at Sheffield Castle, but made frequent visits to Chatsworth, which was one of the large number of houses at their disposal.[13] Lord Shrewsbury was a formal, courteous man, but not as self-sacrificing as St Loe and he was jealous of his honour. None the less, he and Bess shared many interests, including that of building. Two new houses, the Lodge at Handsworth, near Sheffield Manor, and a small house for the accommodation of visitors to his baths at Buxton, were built by the Earl, and from 1585 onwards he was to make dramatic alterations to his manor at Worksop. He was initially supportive of his wife's plans for the enlargement of Chatsworth (**9**).

These plans reflected Bess's increasingly secure financial position, which was independent of that of her husband,[14] and they embodied her social aspirations for herself and her children. She and Lord Shrewsbury were intimate with the leading men of the day who, during the 1570s, were increasingly drawn to the Earl's baths at nearby Buxton, and a suite of state rooms was needed at Chatsworth for their entertainment. Entries in the household books of the 1570s detail the finishing of the new rooms,[15] which, according to the 1601 inventory, were 'very fayre waynscotted with coulorid woodes markentrie and pelasters fayre set foarthe', but of the textile furnishings there is hardly a mention, except for such minor matters as 7d 'payed for the makyng of ij dosen and four napkins' in the week beginning 9 June 1578.[16] The absence of information about the furnishings is

8 George Talbot, 6th Earl of Shrewsbury (1527–90). Fourth husband of Bess, whom he married as his second wife in 1567. His appointment as custodian of Mary Queen of Scots in February 1568/9 placed the marriage under a strain that eventually resulted in separation. *NTPL*

9 Needlework cushion of the *platt of Chatesworth house*, which was in the Gallery at Hardwick in 1601. It shows the house at Chatsworth with the additional storey containing state rooms that Bess added in the early 1570s. The fountain in the inner court is visible through the central arch. *Devonshire Collection*

frustrating, for most of the surviving sixteenth-century textiles at Hardwick date from this time, including some which featured in the great quarrel that developed between Bess and her husband in the late 1570s. The breakdown of the marriage has been blamed on Bess's building programme at Chatsworth and her ambitions for her children, but the primary cause was surely the imposition on the couple of Mary Queen of Scots after fewer than eighteen months of marriage.

Mary, who had fled from imprisonment in Scotland where her infant son James had been declared king in her place, now posed a threat to Queen Elizabeth by providing a focus for the intrigues of the Catholic faction. She was placed in Shrewsbury's charge in February 1568/9 and for most of the following decade she and Lady Shrewsbury were on good terms. However, Mary was confined under a draconian set of regulations which imprisoned Shrewsbury as effectively as they imprisoned her, restricting his movements, even between his own houses, without Queen Elizabeth's express permission, and isolating him from his family and friends. When, in January 1572/3, Shrewsbury was summoned to Court, Sir Ralph Sadler was sent to hold the fort, and within a month, he was complaining that 'I was never so weary of any service as I of this'.[17] Lord Shrewsbury had to stick it for another eleven years, and Bess, although she was often with him at Sheffield and his other houses, spent an increasing amount of time at Chatsworth, whither both she and the Earl sought, more often than Queen Elizabeth would permit, to take the Queen of Scots.

By the late 1570s Shrewsbury was a sick man, heartily tired of his troublesome charge, her intrigues and the hurtful doubts expressed about his own loyalty. It is not surprising that he developed something of a persecution complex which became focused on money and possessions, his wife, her house at Chatsworth and her embroiderers, whom he one night caused to be locked out of Sheffield Lodge. When his son Gilbert sought to reason with him, he broke out, uttering 'cruell words agaynst Owen [Bess's groom] chefely and the imbroderers, ouer longe to trouble your La. w^th'. On that occasion, Gilbert was able to talk his father round and Shrewsbury finally declared that 'her love hathe bene great to me; and myne hathe bene & is as great to her', ending, 'how often I have curced the buyldinge at Chatsworthe, for want of her companye'.[18]

Sadly, the Earl's paranoia increased and the combined efforts of Sir Francis Walsingham, the Earl of Leicester, Lord Burghley and Queen Elizabeth herself could not bring about a reconciliation between him and his wife. Following a review of their claims and counter-claims over their disputed possessions, the Privy Council found in Bess's favour in April 1585. The verdict, which Lord Shrewsbury refused to accept, depended mainly on the existence of a deed of gift concerning Chatsworth and its contents made between the two parties in 1572.[19] A second enquiry was held and judged by Walsingham and Burghley in May 1586; they too found in Bess's favour, but this time Shrewsbury was allowed to sue her son William Cavendish for having come to Chatsworth 'by night and convey[ed] away the principal stuff, and that on two occasions'.[20]

Given the constant toing and froing between their various houses with the Scottish Queen,[21] it is not surprising that the furnishings owned by the Cavendish and Talbot families had become completely mixed. It was perhaps as a result of his growing concern that Lord Shrewsbury had a new inventory taken of Sheffield Castle in 1582, which gives some idea of how furnishings were moved about. It lists tapestries 'brought from London' (either from Shrewsbury House in Chelsea or one of the two houses in the City), one of which had been left 'for to be mended' at Wingfield, a Shrewsbury house in Derbyshire. There were other hangings of forrest work from Hardwick, and twenty pairs of harden sheets which had come from Worksop – yet another of the Earl's houses.[22]

Shrewsbury produced his list of missing goods on 1 August 1586 and Bess's crisp response is dated 4 August; it would make amusing reading were the occasion for it not so sad.[23] Most of the plate had been at Chatsworth at the time of the 1572 deed of gift, so belonged to the Cavendishes. Other items, 'not worth 30s' had been 'stolen by a foot-boy', while yet others had been 'bought by the Earl of purpose for the Countess to give away, which she did, as his Lordship well knoweth'. The lesser textiles were soon dealt with: two pairs of cambric (fine linen) sheets, six pairs of pillowberes and six cupboard-cloths had been made seventeen years before and were worn out. Twenty feather beds and all their furnishings, which had come from the Earl's house at Coldharbour in London and had numbered only twelve in the first place, were spoilt and worn out, being only common beds for servants, while in their place, much better beds had been sent to the Earl's houses at Tutbury, Wingfield and Buxton and were never returned. In her turn, Bess claimed that the Earl had consumed 'better than 1,000l. worth of linen . . . being carried to sundry of his houses to serve his lordship's turn. And, with his often being at Chatsworth with his charge [Mary Queen of Scots], and most of the stuff there spoiled.'[24]

Shrewsbury also laid claim to several sets of wall hangings, including six 'of green leaves', which, according to Bess, had been exchanged for others nineteen years earlier and anyway were covered by the 1572 deed. Also covered by the deed were 'rich hangings 8 pieces which were Sir William Pickering's', for which the Earl claimed he had paid £200. Bess maintained that they had been bought for her for 'nine score pounds' (£180). The most important hangings to feature in the dispute, however, were:

> First, rich hangings made by Thomas Lane, Ambrose, William Barlow, and Henry, Mr Cavendish's man, and had copes of tissue, cloth of gold, and other things towards the making thereof, meat, drink and wages paid to the embroiderers by the Earl during the working of them; and other hangings of green velvet, birds and fowls and needlework set upon velvet.

Bess rejected the Earl's claim, stating that the copes had been bought by Sir William St Loe and were at Chatsworth at the time of the deed of gift. Most of the hangings were made at Chatsworth, and her 'grooms, women, and some boys I kept wrought the most part of them. Never had but one embroiderer at one time that wrought on them. His Lordship never gave the worth of 5l. towards the making of them.'[25]

Neither Bess nor Shrewsbury wanted to concede victory but a begrudging truce was reached against the background of greater events: in October 1586 Mary Queen of Scots was brought to trial and condemned to death. It was Lord Shrewsbury, as Lord Marshal, who gave the order for her execution on 8 February 1587. In April, however, Bess and Shrewsbury were again brought before Queen Elizabeth, and some semblance of a reconciliation enforced. They left together for Wingfield Manor on 22 April 1587, but although Bess seems to have made every effort to restore the marriage, they soon drifted apart. None the less, when Queen Elizabeth wrote to commiserate with Gilbert Talbot on the death of his father in November 1590, she also asked him to 'commend us we pray you to your mother-in-lawe whome thoughe somme others did not so thincke, yet we did knowe and were allway persuaded, would not a lyttle grieve at this hir losse.'[26]

Chapter Two

HARDWICK NEW HALL AND THE 1601 INVENTORY

Bess was nearing 60 when, following an attempt by Lord Shrewsbury to gain forcible entry into Chatsworth, she moved to Hardwick in July 1584. She had bought the Old Hall in the name of her second son William in 1583, from the official receivers of the estate of her bankrupt brother. After the settlement of 1587 and the restoration of the revenues taken by Lord Shrewsbury, Bess embarked on an increasingly ambitious programme of repair and new building at the Old Hall.[1] Within three years, however, the foundations of a New Hall (**10**) had been dug (November 1590), and in 1593 a start was made on a smaller house at Oldcotes, some four miles away. An amazing decade of activity was completed by the building, between 1598 and 1601, of her almshouses at Derby.

The reasons for this activity centred on Bess's ambitions for her heirs and the importance of owning a magnificent house to demonstrate the family's status. Old Hardwick, despite its superb position, was no match for Chatsworth, which had been entailed on her unsatisfactory eldest son Henry, who had not only sided with Shrewsbury in the great quarrel but had declared his illegitimate son as his heir. This was unacceptable to Bess, who now put her energies into the promotion of her favourite son William; he could not have Chatsworth, but he could have Hardwick, not only rebuilt but new-built.

Bess was well aware of Sir Francis Willoughby's great new house at Wollaton in Nottinghamshire, on which some of her own workmen were employed, and rivalry was perhaps another factor; the New Hall would be a designed house, built as a single exercise, not over a period of nearly thirty years as Chatsworth had been. The house was perhaps originally planned with an eye on her dynastic ambitions, whether covert or admitted, for her granddaughter, Arbella, who was related to the Crown through her father, Charles Stuart.[2]

The building of the New Hall is well documented and has been the subject of several studies, including Mark Girouard's assessment of it in relation to the career of Robert Smythson. Bess would have known about Smythson through the work he had done at Longleat in Wiltshire and at Wollaton for her friends Sir John Thynne and Sir Francis Willoughby. She may also have met him during the early planning stages at Worksop, before the quarrel with her husband intensified. It is not known how far Smythson was involved in the details of the interior of the New Hall, but one key figure in its creation was undoubtedly the multi-talented John Balechouse. He had worked for Bess since at least May 1578, when his name appears in a household book; in December 1589 he was at Hardwick, but on board wages, indicating that he was away from his usual station. Once work on the New Hall had started, however, he acted as the overseer, responsible directly to Bess, signing the accounts in her absence and sufficiently in her confidence to make decisions on his own authority.

As the shell of the house took shape, Bess and John Balechouse, in discussion with other of her craftsmen, must have planned and prepared for its internal decoration, both

10 The New Hall at Hardwick viewed from the west with the initials ES for Elizabeth Shrewsbury showing clearly against the sky. The long windows in the right-hand half of the upper storey are those of the Best Bed Chamber, the State Withdrawing Chamber and the High Great Chamber. Bess's private rooms were below them on the first floor. *NTPL/Nick Meers*

fixed – in the form of carved stone, moulded plaster and woodwork – and loose – in the form of textiles and leather. In many cases these had to be planned together and it has been suggested that the size of the High Great Chamber was dictated by the dimensions of the Ulysses tapestries which cover all but the window walls. They certainly form part of a carefully planned interior, although they do not in fact fit very well, being hung in the wrong order so as not to obscure the three doorways completely, and they overhang the panelling below them.

A better example of textiles dictating a decorative scheme is provided by the Gallery, which, despite the later accretion of portraits, is still dominated by its tapestries: a thirteen-piece set of the *Story of Gideon*, which Bess had bought in July 1592. At 19 feet (5·8m) they are exceptionally high, too high to be hung above any panelling, and there is only a narrow band of wall between them and the originally plain ceiling. The top of the tapestries is exactly matched by that of the two fine chimneypieces (**11**) with their figures of Justice and Mercy, which were installed in 1596 or 1597. The space above is filled with a delicate frieze of strapwork and grotesques painted by John Balechouse shortly before the tapestries were hung in July 1598.

A similarly good fit is illustrated by 'six pieces of tapestry hangings with personages

11 The fireplace and overmantle with an alabaster figure of Justice carved by Thomas Accres, installed in the Gallery in 1597/8. Their 5·8m height exactly matches the *Gideon* tapestries which Bess had bought in London in 1592. The tapestries were hung in July 1598. *NT*

12 The Drawing Room more or less as it was in the 1950s when used by the Duchess Evelyn. The tapestries of *personages and my Ladies Armes* are those installed in 1597 when the room was Bess's Withdrawing Chamber. Only one painted shield remains of those that once covered the arms of the original owner, Sir Christopher Hatton. *NTPL/Andy Tryner*

and my ladies Arms in them', which still hang above the panelling in 'my Ladies with drawinge Chamber' (now the Drawing Room). They exactly fill the space which must have been designed to take them (**12**). They are an early example of the English preference for tapestries that could be hung above deep panelling, a preference sufficiently strong for Flemish weavers to produce shallow tapestries specifically to satisfy it.[3]

Bess's building activities had, however, created quite a problem. Although, as Dowager Countess of Shrewsbury (the Earl had died in 1590), she had the use of Wingfield Manor, where she spent much time in the late 1580s and 1590s, and also Shrewsbury House in Chelsea, she could not draw on any of the Shrewsbury houses for the furnishings that she needed to equip the two halls at Hardwick and William's smaller house at Oldcotes, with which he needed help, despite the land and money already settled on him. Bess had already helped Gilbert Talbot, when he and her daughter Mary moved to a new house in 1575, and when his father, in the first stages of his paranoia, had begrudged parting with even the oldest stuff. As Gilbert complained:

> [he] apoynted him of the wardrop to delyver us the tester and curtaynes of the oulde grene and redde bedd of velvett and satten w[h] your La. did see; and the clothe bedd tester & curtaynes w[h] we now lye in, and ii very oulde counterpoynts of tapestry; and *forbad* him to delyver y[e] bedd of cloth of gould & tawney velvety[t] your Ld. sawe.[4]

Now Bess herself was faced with the need to furnish a hugely increased number of rooms at the Old Hall and the whole of the New Hall. Detailed accounts survive for the building and fitting-out of the two halls, but, except for a few references in the general household accounts, there is very little information about their furnishing;[5] more detailed accounts were probably kept by the Wardrobe staff. Some comparative material exists in the Talbot and other papers, but the main evidence of what was involved lies in the inventories of Chatsworth and the two halls drawn up to accompany Bess's will of 27 April 1601.[6] Together the three houses contained well over two hundred rooms, all equipped to some degree with textile furnishings. The quantities were considerable: at least 26 sets of tapestry and another 26 sets of leather, woven and embroidered hangings. Each of the innumerable beds had a textile roof or tester, usually a headcloth rather than

13 Panelling painted with designs similar to those on some of the stained (painted) textiles. The layout also gives some idea of how decorated textile panels were combined, usually with plain fabrics, to make hangings and other large furnishings. The panelling was probably made originally for the Old Hall. *NTPL / John Hammond*

a headboard, a set of curtains with valances to cover the rods and rings, and sometimes base valances or pants to hang from the base of the bed. There were in addition more than 250 blankets, plus 170 fledges, fustians, flannells and rugs made from different qualities of woollen cloth, as well as 250 coverlets, quilts and counterpoints (counterpanes). Many chairs, stools and benches were upholstered and there were at least 150 cushions for increased comfort and decoration. The houses contained about 40 Turkish carpets, 19 in the New Hall, and more than 70 other table and cupboard carpets made of English turkey-work and of woven fabric either with stitched decoration or trimmed with bobbin lace, braid and fringe. Each house was equipped with a range of linen necessary for functions varying from formal dining to the meanest of household duties.

Much of this vast quantity of stuff had been accumulated over the years, some dating back to the 1550s, or earlier if it was from Northaw, which Cavendish had furnished before he married Bess. At least three complete beds and one set of bed curtains recorded at Chatsworth in 1553 and 1562 are identifiable in the 1601 inventory. Some may have been dismantled to make smaller furnishings and others combined to make new bed sets, possibly including Bess's bed in the Old Hall. This was hung with a mix of purple velvet, crimson satin, red and yellow taffeta and blue and white silk damask, all embroidered with coloured silks and trimmed with braid and fringe. More refined, and certainly all of a piece, was her bed at Chatsworth, which was of black figured velvet and black silk damask trimmed with gold braid and fringe – perhaps newly made when she became a widow. If so, she felt no need to follow suit when she moved into the New Hall, where her bed was made of a fine cloth known as scarlet (see p.30), trimmed with gold braid and fringe – a conscious or unconscious return to the bed that was carved with her and Cavendish's arms and hung with red cloth which featured in the 1553 and 1562 inventories.

The 1553 inventory listed forty-eight tapestries at Chatsworth, but by 1601 not only had that number fallen to twenty-one but there were marked differences between the houses in the use of hangings of any sort. In the State Rooms at Chatsworth and the new wings at Hardwick Old Hall, many of the rooms were fitted out with panelling (**13**). There was a total of thirty such rooms at Chatsworth, six of them 'waynscotted to the heighte', that is, to the full height of the room – precluding any need for textile hangings. The Old Hall had twelve rooms 'waynscotted to the top', two with 'waynscott rownde aboute', and seven with it only under the windows; six rooms were hung with tapestries, two with fabric and two with leather. At the New Hall, however, none of the rooms was panelled to the ceiling, thirteen had panelling only below the windows and eight were panelled 'rownde aboute'. There were, however, fifteen sets of tapestry, six of embroidery, three of fabric, one of stained work and one of leather.

These differences do not simply reflect personal preferences or developments in interior design. In the 1590s Bess did not have on call woodworkers of the calibre of those who had worked on the new rooms at Chatsworth in the 1570s; consequently neither hall at Hardwick had any marquetry work and the New Hall had simpler panelling than the Old.[7] The joiner responsible for the New Hall panelling, 'Old Bramley', was criticised for his 'unperfect' work and had to correct mistakes in the High Great Chamber at his own expense.[8] With time at a premium, it was also quicker, but not cheaper, to use textiles. Even at Chatsworth some of the grandest rooms had been left without panelling, including Lord Leicester's Chamber and Withdrawing Chamber, the Low Great Chamber and the Withdrawing Chamber of the Scotch Queen. These had been hung with tapestry and embroidered hangings (**14**), all of which were prized more highly than the finest inlaid woodwork; these textiles had made up the 'principal stuff' carried away from Chatsworth

14 The personification of Chastity from the large appliqué hanging of Lucretia, one of a set of five made for the state apartments at Chatsworth in the early 1570s. The figure holds a sprig of myrtle and is accompanied by a unicorn, both symbols of purity. (Height of figure: 83cm) Inv. T/231b
NTPL/John Hammond

by William Cavendish in 1584 (see p.14), and in 1601 they were among the listed furnishings of the State Rooms at the New Hall.

The State Rooms at Chatsworth were left virtually empty, although the two lower floors remained adequately furnished for the use of various members of the family, including Bess. In 1601, the Middle Wardrobe contained a small quantity of spare furnishings, including four pieces of tapestry, but the other three wardrobes and the storage presses in the maids' room had been emptied and the contents transferred to Hardwick. This must have been quite an undertaking, but, apart from extra money paid to Ellen Steward, the housekeeper at Chatsworth, for unknown duties in June 1594,[9] the only record is a stray note, in Bess's own hand: 'geuen to fore boys that came from Chattesworthe wth mattresses xiid', in September 1599.[10]

The same was true at the Old Hall, although it continued in full use for the accommodation of the servants and any over-spill of visitors from the New Hall, which had a relatively small number of bedrooms. The Wardrobe within William Cavendish's suite of rooms was empty – its contents no doubt transferred to his new house at Oldcotes – and the main Wardrobe, the Low Wardrobe and their adjacent rooms were severely depleted. They still contained five sets of bed hangings, a fair amount of bedding and some turkey-work stool covers, but there were no tapestries or other wall hangings, with the exception of '3 old grene hangings' and fifty-one 'peeces of guilt lether wrought' and thirty-four of 'guilt lether silvered but not finished'. Their unfinished as well as unused state is interesting, for fitted wall panels of decorated leather were expensive items usually imported from the Low Countries, as in 1579, when one of Lord Shrewsbury's ships, which had taken Derbyshire lead to Rouen, made the return journey loaded with wine and leather hangings.[11] Peter Thornton has suggested that the unfinished panels at Hardwick were for use in repairing damaged pieces, but the quantity seems excessive and one wonders whether Bess had once had a skilled leather-worker in her employ.[12] At all events, only a single room in the New Hall was hung with this fashionable and expensive material.

Tapestries

The resources of Chatsworth and the Old Hall notwithstanding, Bess had to find a substantial quantity of material for the New Hall, particularly to cover its walls, even though many were to remain bare, notably those of the main staircase. Sheer quantity was one problem, availability another, as Gilbert Talbot had found in 1576 when looking for hangings for his father's house at Buxton. He wrote from London for the exact measurements, explaining that, although 'very fair hangings may be had at 5s the [measuring] stick, I have not yet seen none that I think deep enough for a great chamber'.[13]

The Gideon tapestries acquired for the New Hall Gallery (15) had belonged to the Lord Chancellor, Sir Christopher Hatton (d.1591), who, in a vain attempt to attract a visit from Queen Elizabeth, had run up enormous debts in building and furnishing his great house at Holdenby in Northamptonshire. Bess may have felt some sympathy for Sir Christopher, but it was very convenient to be able to buy second-hand from his heir, Sir William Hatton, the exceptionally large tapestries which he had expensively commissioned to be woven with his arms. Not only did Bess get them at a good price, but she had the total cost of £326 15s 9d reduced by £5 9s 9d 'for makinge of newe Armes'.[14] In the end she simply covered Sir Christopher's arms with painted wool (16), which cost her 30s 4d, another good example of her careful housekeeping.[15] The purchase is recorded in

an account book that covers Bess's long last visit to London from November 1591 to the end of July 1592. This also contains details of the purchase of the four *Abraham* tapestries (now in the Green Velvet Room), which were to serve as a second set for the Withdrawing Chamber. They were bought in dribs and drabs: three were acquired from the merchant Mulmaster on 6 March and 20 April 1592, as probably was the fourth, which she purchased on the same day as the Gideon set.[16]

A second account book, kept by Bess's London steward Edmund Whalley, records the purchase of three other sets of tapestry in July and October 1591. One was a five-piece set of the *Story of Tobit*, which gave its name to Tobies Chamber in the New Hall; it cost £38 17s and was temporarily installed at Shrewsbury House in Chelsea where Bess lived when not at Court. Acquired at the same time from a merchant, possibly William de Miliner, was a set of sixteen pieces of the *Story of Nathan*, which cost £96 18s, and three months later Whalley bought five pieces 'of courser hangings of varders [verdures]', at the cheap price of only £8 8s.[17]

The set with 'personages and my ladies Armes' in Bess's Withdrawing Chamber had also belonged to Sir Christopher Hatton, but details of its purchase have not survived. Nor is there any record of the acquisition of the *Ulysses* set (**17**) in the High Great Chamber, which was clearly important to Bess.[18] The number of pieces in it and their quality suggest that it may be the set of 'eight rich hangings' purchased from Sir William Pickering before 1572, which featured in the quarrel between Bess and Lord Shrewsbury and which had cost either £180 or £200 (see p.15).[19] The price is right for the size and quality of the set.

All Bess's tapestries were woven in Flanders, and their price per Flemish ell varied according to the complexity of the design, the quality of the weave and the materials

15 (*left*) View of the Gallery showing the thirteen-pieces of tapestry with the *Story of Gideon*, woven for Sir Christopher Hatton in 1578. Bess bought them in 1592 from his heir, Sir William Hatton. Inv. T/82 a-m
NTPL/Graham Challifour

16 (*above*) A panel of felted wool with painted arms, which was used to cover those of Sir Christopher Hatton on the Gideon tapestries. (24 × 21cm) Inv. T/408 *SML*

PIVM DECVS VLIX · PARENTEM VTRVMQVE CHA
RISS CONIVGI TROIAM PETITVRVS COMMENDAT

17 *Ulysses saying farewell to his family*, from a set of eight mid-16th century Flemish tapestries. Ulysses is shown placing his wife, Penelope, in the care of his parents. His name is woven on his belt and the P and final E of Penelope are visible on the hem of her skirt. (366 × 255 cm) Inv. T/83c *NTPL/John Hammond*

used. Figure subjects, which required skilful weaving, particularly of the faces, cost a great deal more than simple verdures, while all-wool tapestries were cheaper than those incorporating silk or gold and silver threads. Some of the forty-eight tapestries recorded at Chatsworth in 1553 had silk highlights, but none contained metal threads, and of those bought in the 1590s, only the *Abraham* set was enhanced with gold. In fact, the gold was confined to a single piece, which cost 20s per ell, while the other three cost 14s per ell. This was still a high figure compared to 7s for the *Tobit* set, 6s 6d for the *Gideons*, 6s for the sixteen-piece set of *Nathan* and 1s 6d for the cheap set of verdures.

The pieces that form the *Abraham* set (**18**) probably came from two weavings,[20] one with and one without metal thread, of a simplified and smaller-scale version of a popular twelve-piece set designed by Bernard Van Orley and first woven by William Pannemaker of Brussels around 1540. Henry VIII had a full set, which still hangs at Hampton Court Palace, with which Bess must have been familiar. The prices paid for the Abrahams suggest that they were new, since they fit with those of tapestries seen at Antwerp in September 1591 by Michael Moody, acting as an agent for the Earl of Essex: 'I have

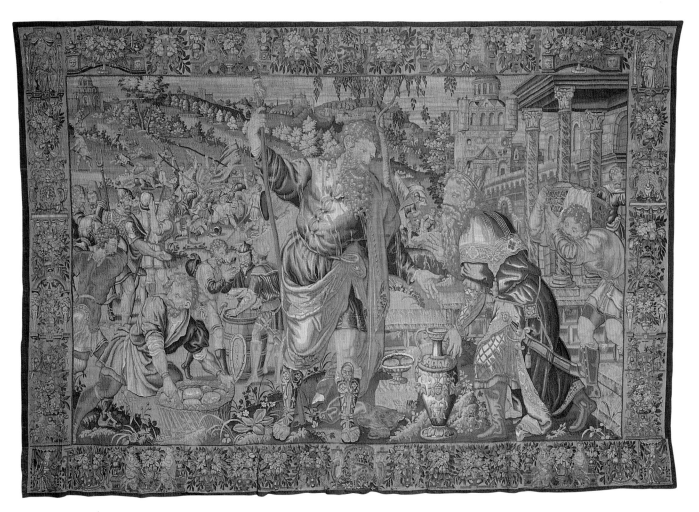

provided a suit or two of the most fairest hangings that are in this country. The one suit is the story of Cyrus, 8 pieces of six Flemish ells deep, the lowest price I can drive them unto is nine florins an ell, which is 18s English. . . . These are here in Antwerp for I can find no such choice in Brussels.'[21]

Bess paid less than half as much per ell for her other sets, but she still spent the large sum of £556 and, if £180 or £200 is added for the Sir William Pickering set (see p.15) and a token amount for the 'personages with my ladies Armes', the total rises to nearer £800. This accounts for only a third of the sets, or fifty-one of the 118 tapestries in the Old and New Halls, but she had, none the less, spent wisely and the one expensive set was balanced by some reasonably priced, good-quality pieces and two huge sets at bargain prices. The sixteen pieces of Nathan seem to have been divided between three adjacent rooms in the Old Hall, all of which had 'hangings with Personages' of the same depth, and the five-piece set of verdures seems likely to be one of the two sets recorded there.

The other five sets bought in London in 1591–2 were installed in the New Hall, where, with the exception of the Tobit tapestries, they still hang, together with a five-piece set of *The Planets*, which has been returned to its original setting (now the Blue Bedroom), and two pieces from a four-piece set of *The Prodigal Son*, which was at Chatsworth in the 1560s.[22] Two more sets of Old Testament stories were recorded in 1601 but are no longer identifiable. One, of the *Story of Jacob*, gave its name to 'Jacob's Chamber',[23] and the other, an eight-piece set of the *Story of David*, hung in the Low Great Chamber. This must have been of good quality and, unless it had been formed by adding one piece to the seven tapestries of *David and Bathsheba* recorded at Chatsworth in the 1560s, it would be another candidate for the set acquired from Sir William Pickering.

The eight-piece set now in the Withdrawing Chamber was for several years referred to

18 *Abraham receiving bread and wine for his soldiers from the priest, Melchisadek*, from a set of four tapestries of the *Story of Abraham* which Bess bought in 1592. All four are finely woven with silk highlights, but one of them, not this one, is also enhanced with gold thread – an extravagance rather unusual for Bess. (340 × 490cm) Inv. T/76c NTPL/John Hammond

19 Fragment of an early 16th-century Flemish tapestry of a lion hunt. This is one of the tapestries that Sir William Cavendish may have acquired before he married Bess. (Detail: 145 × 86cm) Inv. T/97 *NTPL/John Hammond*

as the 'David set', simply because it matches the 1601 description in number and size. In reality, it shows scenes from the story of Scipio Africanus and the Second Punic War. It does not appear in the inventories, although it does date from the second half of the sixteenth century and was presumably at Oldcotes or the London house in 1601. It, too, is of good enough quality and contains the right number of pieces to be a possible contender for the Sir William Pickering set.

An early sixteenth-century tapestry, now on the staircase above the door into the High Great Chamber, also relates to the *Story of David*, although it shows David's son Solomon being crowned and ordering the building of the Temple of Jerusalem. One other early sixteenth-century tapestry hangs lower down on the staircase: a fragment of a lion-hunt (**19**) from a set known by various names, including *The Voyage to Calcutta* and *The Portuguese and Indies*. The history of these two tapestries is not known, but they could have been acquired by the upwardly mobile Sir William Cavendish before or during his marriage to Bess. If so, they must have been moved from Northaw or the London house to Chatsworth and then to Hardwick, perhaps before 1601 if the piece on the top landing is part of the set from the Low Great Chamber, or subsequently during one of the major reorganisations. It is also possible that the four famous Devonshire *Hunting Tapestries*, now in the Victoria and Albert Museum, and which date from the second quarter of the fifteenth century, followed the same route. There were six very large 'hangings of Personages with Forrest Work' in the New Hall, four in the Hall and two in Bess's Bedchamber.[24] Their grandeur, as well as their association with William Cavendish, would have endeared them to Bess.

The mixed set of *Heroes* which had been in Tymme's Chamber at Chatsworth in the 1560s, may have been split up in the 1590s, with one of the David pieces joining the set in the Low Great Chamber at Hardwick and the *Judgement of Solomon* remaining to complete the 'ffyve peeces of tapisterie hanginges of the storie of Salomon', recorded in Tymme's Chamber in 1601. Alternatively, all the pieces had remained there and were inaccurately described by a clerk who recognised only one of the scenes. Certainly the full set does not match in size or number any of the anonymous sets of 'Personages' listed in the Old and New Halls in 1601. These will never now be identified, although some of them may survive among the fragmentary pieces still in the New Hall. It is worth noting, however, that there are now far more tapestries in the house than there were in 1601, for reasons that will be explained in subsequent chapters.[25]

Carpets

In the 1590s, Bess bought not only tapestries but also plate from Sir William Hatton. It would be interesting to know whether, having stopped to see Holdenby on her way back from London in August 1592, she later negotiated for other furnishings, including carpets, as Gilbert Godfrey sought to do. He wrote in August 1593 to Sir Robert Cecil asking him 'to move Sir William Hatton for a Turkey Carpet of seven yards and a half long and some other things which he hath at Holdenby'.[26] It is not known how big a price difference there was between a second-hand and a new carpet, but in November 1602 a Mr Browne wrote to Sir Robert Sidney telling him that he had 'bought a Turkey carpet for my Lord Bergavenny, seven Dutch ells long; it cost £27 sterling but it is esteemed very fine, and well worth the money.'[27] There is nothing to indicate the origins of the 'Turkey' (Turkish) carpets recorded in the 1601 inventories, but the two large carpets and some of the smaller ones listed in the 1553 inventory of Chatsworth (see p. 10) should have survived, although the risk of damage will have increased as carpets began to be used on the floor rather than spread over tables. By 1601, eight of the thirty-eight Turkey carpets recorded in the three houses were described as floor carpets, of which seven were in the New Hall, together with five of English turkey-work and, most unusually, floor spreads of fledge (coarse wool) and checked crewel (worsted wool).

The inventory clerks seem to have been careful to distinguish between real Turkish carpets (**20**), which they called Turkey or Turkie carpets, and carpets of English turkey-work, although it is probable that they made a mistake in the case of 'a Cubberd, two turkie Carpets for it, one of them with my Ladies Armes', in the Low Great Chamber. English turkey-work was a pile wool fabric, knotted in the Turkish manner but on a warp of linen or hemp, instead of wool. Many of the surviving examples are relatively coarse upholstery panels with patterns closer to English needlework than to oriental carpets (**22**), but finer pieces were also made. The Earl of Leicester, who was something of a carpet buff, owned a 'Turkie carpet of Norwich making',[28] which must have been of good quality, perhaps similar to the four European carpets with oriental patterns at Boughton House in Northamptonshire. Three have borders woven with the arms of Montague impaling Jeffrey and two of them are dated 1584 and 1585 (**21**). An English carpet in the Victoria and Albert Museum also has small coats of arms in the border, and the date 1603, although its design is based on the small-pattern Holbein carpets. Sixteenth-century oriental carpets with English arms do survive, but only from Persia and India, not from Turkey.[29] In addition, for Bess to have commissioned a Turkish carpet to be woven with her arms seems out of character, while a good copy at a lower price is the sort of bargain she enjoyed – on a par with putting painted coats of arms on the Gideon and other second-hand tapestries.

Norwich is known to have been a centre for the production of turkey-work, but there is no information about the size or organisation of the industry.[30] The Hardwick records

20 An Anatolian knotted-pile carpet of the second half of the 16th-century with a star Ushak pattern. (330 × 190cm) Inv. T/95 *NTPL/John Hammond*

21 (*right*) Detail of a fine European knotted-pile carpet with a design based on those of star Ushak carpets (fig. **20**). In the border is a small shield with the arms of Montague impaling Jeffrey and the date 1585. (Width: 183cm) *Buccleuch Collection*.

22 (*below*) Turkey-work stool cover cut from an English knotted-pile carpet of the late 16th century. The pattern of zig-zags with leaves and berries is related to contemporary English needlework. (Detail of top: 46 × 55cm) Inv. F/335 *NTPL/John Hammond*

do, however, provide some evidence that there were itinerant carpet-weavers, as well as embroiderers and tapestry-weavers. Payment was made in October 1592 to a carpet-weaver named Beard,[31] and the 1601 inventory records 'a frame to weyve [weave] carpets', in a 'small vault' at Chatsworth.

Bess would have acquired real Turkish carpets as need and opportunity occurred, and it has been suggested that some of these were brought back by her son Henry Cavendish, who travelled to Constantinople (now Istanbul) in 1589,[32] but in addition to the second-hand market, a more likely source was her husband, the Earl of Shrewsbury.[33] Although he traded mainly in Europe, he was in close contact with the leading London merchants Sir Richard Staper and Sir Edward Osborne, who established direct trading links with the Levant during the 1570s, just as Chatsworth was being enlarged. In a surviving letter of September 1585, Sir Edward wrote to inform Lord Shrewsbury of the arrival of a ship from Turkey laden with carpets which he thought might be of interest,[34] and although by then the Earl would not have been buying on behalf of his wife, her son William, who was also involved in overseas trade, had probably taken over this role.

India and the Far East

Carpets were not the only oriental goods recorded at Hardwick: there was a 'quilt of india stuff imbrodered with beastes', in the Little Chamber within the Best Bedchamber, and a second one in the Wardrobe 'of yellow stuffe imbrodered with birdes and beastes'. Although brief, these descriptions raise a number of interesting questions. Surviving Indian coverlets of the late sixteenth and early seventeenth centuries, including one at Hardwick, have grounds not of 'yellow stuffe', but of white cotton. 'Stuff' was a catch-all word sometimes applied more specifically to worsted wools, while embroidery, as will be explained, was a precise technical term that did not include stitched linen/cotton, but did encompass appliqué. It is just possible, therefore, that the two coverlets at Hardwick

in 1601 had grounds of fairly thick dyed cotton decorated with applied motifs cut from plain, printed or painted cotton. Had they survived they would have been very rare indeed, since such work was generally made for the domestic Indian market and not normally exported.

There are two Indian coverlets still in the house, one of which can be dated by its design to the early eighteenth century. The other was made in Bengal in the late sixteenth or early seventeenth century (**23**). It has a thin layer of wadding sandwiched between layers of white cotton and is worked through all the layers with red, blue, green and orange silk in running stitches. Apart from a central rosette surrounded by concentric rings, the ground is divided by straight bands into a series of rectangles, and these are filled with scenes of men and women, birds and animals, surrounded by flowers and geometric ornaments. It is early enough to be one of the coverlets listed in the 1601 inventory – although wrongly described by the clerks – or was perhaps acquired slightly later by Bess's son William, who was directly involved with the East India Company, founded in 1600. Other textiles came from even further away. The only two cushions at Hardwick that survive complete in every detail are a pair 'of Crimson sattin imbrodered with Straweberries and wormes with blewe silk frenge and tassells & lyned with blue damaske' (**24**); the damask was woven in China, but there is no information about its cost or how it was acquired.

Yardage Fabric

The majority of the furnishings in the house, from bed-sets to cushions, were not bought ready-made however; they were constructed from imported European silks and wool and linen cloth either from England or abroad. The work was done either by members of the household or, in the case of complex beds and upholstered furniture, by a professional furnisher or upholsterer. The surviving account books do not provide full

23 (*left*) Detail from the border area of a large, late 16th-century coverlet from Bengal. The coverlet has a thin layer of wadding between two layers of white cotton and is closely stitched through all the layers with red, blue, green and orange silk. The centre is decorated with figurative and geometric ornaments. Inv. T/139
NTPL/John Hammond

24 (*above*) Detail from one of a pair of long cushions showing the 16th-century Chinese silk damask used for the backs. Its colour is echoed in the short silk fringe trimming the edges and the large tassel. For the front, see fig. **59**. Inv. T/396 *NTPL/John Hammond*

details for the making of any particular item but, as the component parts were paid for separately, it is possible to suggest their likely cost.

During her last visit to London Bess bought enormous quantities of fabric, mostly from the mercer John Smythe. Some of this included lengths as long as 20 yards of satin at 12s 2d the yard and 27 yards of black velvet at 20s the yard, which were intended for clothing; witness such precise descriptions as '28 yards of black stuff for two gowns at 4s the yard'.[35] As noted above, 'stuff' was a generic term for worsted, that is, cloth woven from long-staple combed wool, while the term 'woollens' denoted fabric made from short-staple carded wool. Like almost all fabrics, they were used interchangeably for both clothing and furnishings.

An extensive range of wool fabric was available: 6d a yard was paid in October 1599 for an unspecified type of crimson cloth to cover stools at the Derby Almshouses, while 'bays', a napped fabric with a worsted warp and a woollen weft, varied in price from 2s to 3s 8d a yard.[36] Bess had five inner curtains of purple bays on her own bed in the New Hall, but the outer hangings of scarlet would have been much more expensive. Scarlet was a very high quality woollen cloth which, although usually dyed scarlet-red (itself an expensive colour), was sometimes found in black or other colours. Bess bought two small pieces of scarlet while in London in 1591–2, which cost 40s and 50s a yard – more than twice as expensive per yard as silk velvet, although probably of a greater width.[37] More typical of the middle-quality wools used for furnishing was penistone, a local wool from Penistone in west Yorkshire. This has been described as a coarse cloth, sometimes napped and felted, but Bess paid as much as 4s 8d a yard for some green penistone in 1599, which may have been that used for the 'too curtins of grene penistone' that hung in the Low Great Chamber in 1601.[38] Cheaper than penistone was mockado, a woollen fabric woven with a short pile. Bess paid 2s a yard for red mockado in 1592 and, in 1601, 2s 8d a yard for 27½ yards of 'stryped mockeadowe . . . orrynge tawny and grene'.[39] In 1601 there were hangings of red mockado in the closet by the Pearl Bedchamber and in store in the Old Hall were five bed curtains, also of red mockado, perhaps the set recorded at Chatsworth in 1562 (see p.12).[40]

Similar in price to mockado was a closely woven worsted known as draughte work. Prior to Bess's visit to London in 1591, her steward Edmund Whalley bought some for 2s 8d a yard from 'the upholster in Cornewall [Cornwell, London] . . . to serve for wyndow peeces to hange at Chelsey'.[41] More commonly used for window curtains at Hardwick was darnix, one of the many mixed fabrics available. It had a linen warp and a woollen weft and was available in a variety of qualities, with patterns ranging from simple diapers to flowers.

Another mixed fabric used in the house was fustian, made with a linen warp and a cotton weft. Originally imported via Fustat in Egypt, by the sixteenth century it was made throughout Europe, including Lancashire.[42] Prices ranged from 11d the yard for crane-coloured English fustian, to 12d the yard for Jenes (Genoese) fustian 'for lyneing of quilts and other things', to 15d the yard for white holmes fustian from Ulm in Germany.[43] Fustian was used to make a type of blanket called a fustian, as was a coarse wool, called fledge. In 1582, the yardage fabric in store at Sheffield Castle had included 'whoole clothes of fledge to make fledges of, peeces iij'.[44] Woollen cloth was also used: 41½ yards at 15d the yard was bought to make blankets for the Derby Almshouses and elsewhere in September 1599,[45] but, by the late sixteenth century, the finest blankets were being made in Spain. In 1601, Bess had 27 Spanish blankets at the New Hall and two in the Old Hall, but their cost is not recorded.

The main silk fabrics bought for furnishings were satin and velvet. Satin cost between

8s and 12s a yard and was used for bed hangings, counterpoints, table carpets, cushions and covers for chairs.[46] The comfortable chair in Bess's Bedchamber was covered with russet satin trimmed with silver braid and silver and silk fringe, but it was probably not new because it also had a loose cover of 'scarlet imbrodered with flowers of petepoynt [*petit point*]', to match the bed. Also used was 'satin of bridges', a cheaper version with a silk warp and linen weft, woven at, or exported via, Bruges. Bess had bought some in the 1550s at 2s 3d a yard for her litter,[47] but by the 1590s it was used mainly for linings.

In 1599 Bess's steward Timothy Pusey paid £23 for 20 yards of black velvet at 23s the yard, 'w[ch] veluite ys towars the border of the hanging'.[48] The identity of the hanging is uncertain, but the purchase is representative of the huge amounts of black velvet recorded in the inventories, although it was also bought in other colours – white, purple, crimson, green, blue, watchet, orange tawny, russet and murrey – for use on objects as varied as beds, cushions, coffers and book covers. Like the satin, velvet was, with few exceptions, a plain fabric and any decorative effect was achieved by combining it with fabrics of a different colour or texture, by adding braids and fringes or, in the most expensive pieces, by embroidery. Examples include 'a lowe stoole of black and grene velvett and cloth of golde' in the Gallery; 'a chair of crimson velvet layde with golde and silver lace' in the Prodigal Chamber; and 'a long quition [cushion] of black velvet imbrodered with trees of nedlework' in the Withdrawing Chamber. The trees of needlework would have been worked on a canvas ground and then applied, a simple technique used throughout the house. The finest embroidery of metal threads, purl, strip and spangles, was much more complex, as on the bed in Tobies Chamber, which was one of the beds also recorded in the 1553 inventory. It had a tester of 'oring & murry coulored velvet imbrodered with golde and silver twist, double vallans of murry and tawnie velvet with golde, silver and silk fringe, all imbrodered with twyst and the seams layed on with bone [bobbin] lace and armes in the bedes head.' Even more elaborate was the pearl bed of 1547 (see p. 10).

The cost of silk and metal *passementerie* was high (**25**). In November 1599, for example, Bess paid 22s for 'thre ounces of sylvar Lase for bynding lace for a bed', and a total of £2 12s for gold chain lace and mixed braid of metal and silk threads. Between April 1599 and August 1600, Henry Travice, William Cavendish's London steward, spent a further £27 17s 10d on coloured silk binding lace, gold and silver fringe, gold thread, and black and blue silk to be sent to Derbyshire.[49] The cost was high, but nothing like that of metal-thread embroidery. In July 1607 a very fine bed was made for Bess's daughter Mary, who had succeeded her as Lady Shrewsbury. Three bills survive: one is for two great and two small curtains and a headpiece of velvet embroidered with metal thread, strip and purl that came to £85 8s 6d; the second, for the embroidered canopy and valance, came to £153 14s 10½d; and the third, for 190 yards of silver braid, various depths of silver and crimson fringe, silver buttons and loops, crimson ribbon and cord, sewing silk and silk lining fabric, came to £251 6s 8d. The grand total was £490 10s ½d.[50]

Luxurious as many of the furnishings at the New Hall were, they do not suggest conspicuous consumption on that scale. Interestingly, the most valuable pieces seem to date from earlier in Bess's life, notably her marriage bed of 1547, which reflects the extravagant lifestyle of William Cavendish rather than Bess's preference only for that which is 'needful and necessary' (see p. 10). This deep-seated belief in moderation was reflected in the name of her second daughter, Temperance, and perhaps also explains why she substituted Temperance for Charity in the second set of appliqué hangings (see p. 69). These two sets, which now hang in the Hall and on the Chapel Landing, were made using rich textiles salvaged from ecclesiastical vestments (**69**), but little else of equivalent value

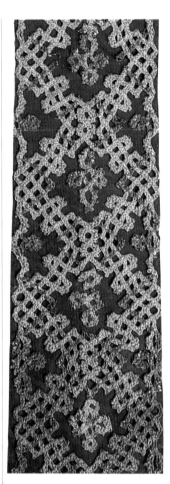

25 Gold and silver bobbin lace dating from the mid-16th century. References to bobbin lace in Bess's account book for 1548–50 are among the earliest known, and her purchase of silk and metal thread for bone (bobbin) lace show that it was already being made in England. (Width: 10cm) Inv. T/442 *SML*

can be identified in the 1601 inventories. With the exception of silk damask, there are very few examples of patterned silks – a bed cover of 'wroughte silke stuffe red and green' in the Gallery Chamber being one – and there are only a few more examples of patterned velvet. These included a set of bed hangings of tinsel and black wrought (patterned) velvet which, together with a matching stool, was in the Wardrobe – suggesting that it was an old set, probably dating from the time of the Cavendish marriage. The same was likely to have been true of the long cushion of black wrought velvet set with silver studs and silver fringe in the Wardrobe of the Old Hall.

The tinsel used in the bed curtains was, like the tissue used in the counterpoint of the best bed, a patterned silk or half-silk fabric elaborated by additional wefts or warps of metal thread. In sixteenth-century inventories they are often classified as cloths of gold or silver, but the specific names denote the method or degree of their elaboration: tinsel was enhanced with metal strip, while tissue (which could also have a velvet ground) was decorated with raised loops of metal thread (**69**).[51] Neither fabric features in the accounts of the 1590s, but Bess did buy 2¼ yards of cloth of silver at 30s the yard.[52] This was the requisite amount for a long cushion and in 1601 there were cushions of cloth of silver in the Low Great Chamber, the Ship Bedchamber and the Wardrobe.

Silk damask features extensively in the inventories. The six hangings in Arbella's room, for example, were of 'yellowe, blewe and other Coulored damask and satten wroughte with golde flowers and trees', but it was more often used to line bed curtains and for the backs of cushions, including the pair mentioned above with backs of imported Chinese damask, the cost of which is unknown (see p.29). In December 1592 Bess bought 50 yards of silk damask from John Smythe at 9s 4d a yard and a further 15 yards at the high price of 14s a yard in the following June.[53]

Used for linings in all types of furnishing were the light silks, sarcenet and taffeta, so alike that their names were sometimes linked together, as in the 'crimson taffetie sarcenet' lining of a table carpet in the High Great Chamber. Both were available in a wide range of colours. Sarcenet could have either a tabby or a twill weave, while taffeta was a tabby weave but with weft threads slightly thicker than the warp, and was often woven with stripes or decorative tufts. In the 1590s, plain and tuft taffeta cost 9-15s a yard.[54]

Although, as suggested, many of the furnishings in the New Hall must have been quite old, an 'olde curtain of red and green saye' in the 'Chamber at the end of the Walke', is about the only item described as such. (Saye or say was a light-weight, twill-woven cloth.) Conversely, very few objects are described as new; they include new ticks for feather beds in the Turrets, a 'new Coverlet of blue cloth stitched with white' in the Stair Chamber (22 yards of blue cloth had been bought for £11 in April 1592[55]) and a covering of 'newe grene cloth with yellow and grene silk frenge and a grene and yellowe lace about it', for the bed in the Green Chamber.

Only in the case of the linen, which – with the plate – was listed separately, was a more precise record made. There was a total of 702½ yards of unused lengths of linen, listed according to their quality, width and purpose: fine damask for table cloths of 2-3 yards wide; diaper for table cloths of 1½-2¼ yards wide; fine diaper for napkins and less fine diaper 'rowde with blue', that is, marked to show where each napkin was to be cut. Finally, there was fine damask, less fine damask and diaper for the towels used at table.

Also in store were made-up table cloths, napkins and towels: 45 long table cloths of damask, diaper and plain linen; 25 square table cloths, one of damask, the rest of diaper; 9 cupboard cloths of damask and 3 of linen. The napkins were counted by the dozen: 6 dozen of damask plus 18 from incomplete sets, 8 dozen of diaper plus 18 odd ones.

Despite the quantity listed, this stock of linen did not represent all that was in the house, but only that of high quality which, like the plate, represented a substantial capital investment. The best guide to its value is provided by the cost of a quantity of linen bought in Rouen by Lord Shrewsbury in 1575. He paid:

£17 6s 4d for 27 ells 2 quarters of fine damask for table cloths [1¾ ells wide] at 12s 6d the ell.

£16 5s 0d for 30 ells of damask for table napkins at 12s 6d the ell.

£9 0s 4d for 22 ells of diaper of Rouen making at 8s 2d the ell.[56]

This made a total of £42 11s 8d for 79½ ells – rather more than one tenth of the unused linen in store at Hardwick.

The purchase of linen is recorded in the account books throughout the 1590s, although its purpose is seldom noted and much must have been for shirts, shifts and other items of clothing. The average cost of plain linen was 1s a yard, although some bought at Chesterfield cost as little as 6d a yard and, on 14 December 1599, 16 yards of linen at 7½d a yard was bought to make 'towe longe haule clothes and one shorte one'.[57] These were for use in the hall at Hardwick where the lower servants ate. The linen was part of an order carefully recorded by Bess herself. In addition to the 16 yards of linen, she bought 10 yards of harden (woven from hemp or other tow) at 9d the yard to make hall cloths of 6 and 4 yards in length, 7 yards of coarse cloth at 5½d the yard, 'wch clothes ys made into for dosyne [4 dozen] of napkins and deleured to Sheldone ... wth the haule clothes before written'.[58] Although relatively new, this table linen does not appear in the 1601 inventory, nor do any of the innumerable sheets and pillow cases or other essential household linen in daily use. The only sheets and pillow cases listed are the exceptionally fine ones in store: 1 pair of very fine cambric sheets, 8 pairs of fine holland sheets and 8 pairs and 1 single sheet that are 'not so fine'. There were also 3 single 'coarse sheets'. Only 3 pillowberes of cambric and 26 holland ones are listed. Cambric, which was used mainly for fine clothing, was relatively expensive; Bess bought 2 ells at 4s 6d the ell in April 1592 and, in July of the same year, seven 'remn'ts of Cambricke all four Ell and a quarter', for £2 8s. Holland varied in quality, but the best could cost as much as 6s an ell.[59] Even more costly was embroidered linen, of which Bess had about 35 pieces in store, all carefully described (see p.43). This was wrapped and stored, with a sweet-bag of changeable taffeta (no doubt containing lavender or some other sweet herb) in five large chests. Their location is not noted, but they may have been among the chests in Bess's own rooms, or perhaps those in the nearby Maids' Chamber, which contained 'foure Iron bound Cofers, nyne trunckes, a wood Chest', together with other coffers and trunks in the Closet.[60] The linen in daily use would have been divided according to its purpose and put in the charge of the relevant household staff such as Sheldone.

The Completed House

The 1601 inventory catches the New Hall at a moment of repose, with the building work and the fitting-out of the State Rooms at last complete. A trick of light can still fleetingly re-create something of the original splendour of the Gallery and High Great Chamber, but elsewhere the changes made over time have been too drastic. The Withdrawing Chamber, for example, has been literally reduced – by the lowering of its ceiling – to an impersonal version of the Drawing Room on the floor below, but in 1601 it provided a magnificent centre point for the suite. Then, as now, there were three points of entry: through a central door opening directly from the Gallery; a small door tucked in a corner

PENELOPE

of the High Great Chamber and probably used only by Bess and her most important guests; and a third door leading into the Best Bedchamber with which it was furnished *en suite*, together with the passage beyond, which led back into the Gallery. The room was as high as the Gallery and High Great Chamber and had a large overmantel, no doubt decorated with strapwork and heraldry.[61] The walls were panelled to a height of 4 feet and above the panelling were the five majestic appliqué hangings of *The Virtues* (see p.68ff), then still glowing with gold and silver, deep reds, blues and greens, set off by backgrounds of black and white velvet (**26**). Despite the provision of the *Abraham* tapestries (see p.24) as an alternative set, it is unlikely that these spectacular pieces were ever moved.[62]

The remains of wall-paintings to either side of the fireplace suggest that the space not covered by the hangings was painted in the same way as the walls between the windows in the High Great Chamber (see fig.**95**), thus providing a visual link between the rooms, and in both there were portraits and paintings hung in the window bays. *The Return of Ulysses to Penelope*, a painting that is now back in the Withdrawing Chamber, would have complemented both the embroidered hanging of Penelope in the same room and the Ulysses tapestries next door. There was also a second painting, *The Prodigal Son*, which seemed to be a favourite subject with Bess, who perhaps still hoped for the reform of her 'bad son Henry'.

The floor was matted and there was also a floor carpet of English turkey-work, but otherwise there was little furniture, since the room was a formal one to which members of a dinner party would temporarily withdraw while the High Great Chamber was cleared and prepared for other entertainment. The Withdrawing Chamber also contained the sea-dog table covered with a needlework carpet depicting David and Saul and trimmed with blue silk and a gold fringe; a cupboard with 'tills' (drawers) – perhaps one of the two that are now in the room – which also had a needlework carpet lined with silk and edged with a gold fringe; and a small table with an inlaid top on which stood a small writing-desk inlaid in white. Little seating was provided for the guests, although there was a needlework chair and velvet-covered footstool decorated with slips, (floral sprigs) for Bess and six stools, four of crimson velvet with applied slips and two inlaid and set with stones in the French style, as well as three low stools of cloth of gold with needlework borders. These would have been for the women, who sometimes also sat on large floor cushions, although there were none at Hardwick.[63] There were three long cushions in the Withdrawing Chamber, one of which, decorated with the *Story of Phaeton*, is still in the house, although it no longer has its gold fringe and tassels of gold and silk (see p.49). A second needlework cushion depicted *Venus and Cupid*, while the third was a very elaborate one of black velvet with needlework trees 'purfled over [highlighted] with gold', which was no doubt for display rather than use.

The main purpose of the Withdrawing Chamber was also for display. It was dominated by the near life-size and sumptuously clothed figures of the Virtues, who looked down on Bess's friends displaying – in person or in their portraits – the spectacular fashions of the final years of the sixteenth century.[64] These were made of the same rich materials found in the furnishings, and were as elaborately decorated, contributing to the colourful impact of late Elizabethan interiors. By 1601, Bess herself was wearing black (**27**), as befitted her age and widowed status, but her clothes were made of the finest velvet, damask and wool, and the dark colours provided a perfect foil for her heavy gold chains and other jewellery, as well as for her ruffs of fine linen.[65] In her younger days, Bess had been more colourfully dressed, as her earliest portrait demonstrates (see fig.**4**). It probably dates from shortly before Cavendish's death in 1557, and shows her expensively dressed in a fur-lined gown

26 Figure of Penelope from one of the five great appliqué hangings that dominated the State Withdrawing Chamber in 1601. Note the grotesque animal mask at the centre of the arch crowned with a pair of coiling, three-dimensional snakes. (Height of figure: 111cm) Inv.T/231a *NTPL/John Hammond*

27 (*right*) Bess as Dowager Countess of Shrewsbury, painted in the 1590s, possibly by Rowland Lockey. She wears a widow's cap and the severity of her black velvet clothes is relieved by the starched ruff and her magnificent four-row string of pearls. *NTPL/Hawkley Studios*

28 (*far right*) Queen Elizabeth I painted by an unknown artist *c.*1599. The decoration on her skirt and stomacher is probably painted on white satin (see fig. **74**). Note the chair with its embroidered back and the long cushion laid across its arms. *NTPL/Hawkley Studios*

with patterned guards and fastened with gold aglets, a French hood decorated with pearls and a gold billament set with diamonds, a superb pair of jewelled bracelets and a linen smock embroidered with red silk. The purchase of woven silks, as well as silk thread for the decoration of her and Cavendish's linen is recorded in the earliest of the account books (1548–50) but, by the end of the 1590s, the richest materials and embroideries recorded were those she purchased as New Years' gifts for the Queen.[66]

In 1591-2, for example, she paid the large sum of £50 to the Queen's embroiderer, John Parr, to work the pieces of a gown for the Queen, which was made up by William Jones, the Queen's tailor, for a further £50.[67] It is not possible to link this gift with the portrait of Elizabeth that hangs in the Gallery (**28**), since this shows the Queen dressed in fashions of the late 1590s, and it is not the velvet gown but the spectacular petticoat, with its motifs of plants and sea monsters, that suggests a link with Bess. The Queen is known to have welcomed richly decorated garments and accessories, so it is more than likely that Bess made a second such gift. A payment of £50 was made to William Jones on 6 March 1600/1, but there is no record of a matching payment to John Parr, nor a surviving gift roll to settle the point.[68]

Queen Elizabeth never went to Hardwick, although the State Rooms had probably been built in the hope of such a visit and her arms were prominently displayed on the overmantel of the High Great Chamber. The rooms were none the less reserved for

29 The Dining Room, which was built as the Low Great Chamber for dining and recreation. The chair in the front left corner is one of several dining chairs upholstered in satin-weave horsehair, probably from Norwich. *NTPL/Graham Challifour*

formal functions and the day-to-day life of the household took place mainly on the two lower floors. Even here, however, distinctions of rank had their place. One important room on the first floor was the Low Great Chamber, now the Dining Room. Both Chatsworth and the Old Hall had such rooms, but they had resulted from Bess's enlargements, whereas at the New Hall the room was planned from the start. Perhaps they had proved both practical and popular as grand rooms to be used by the upper servants for dining and recreation. Bess, her gentlewomen and her immediate family ate in the adjoining Little Dining Chamber (the Paved Room) when not dining formally in the High Great Chamber.

In 1601, the Low Great Chamber (**29**) was hung with eight fine tapestries of the *Story of David*, all 11 feet deep. There was no panelling, except below the windows, and the space above the tapestries was bare except for twelve wooden panels 'set with Arms', either weapons or coats of arms. The floor was matted, but there was also a turkey-work carpet on the floor, indicating the status of those who used the room. The furniture related primarily to dining. There was a cupboard – that is, a two-tiered stand for cups (goblets) from which the wine was served – with two Turkish carpets, one for each of its shelves. There was one long, carved and inlaid table, which also had two turkey carpets, for alternative use, or to lie end to end, and two smaller, square tables, one with a Turkish carpet and the other with an inlaid top in black and white, set with marble stones, which had certainly come from Chatsworth, together with other similarly decorated furniture.

Seating was provided for the tables and also for more informal purposes; there were three large and two small chairs, eight stools, four forms and one low and one little stool. All had textile covers, and one group, comprising a chair, three forms, a low stool and a cushion, which was covered with cloth of gold or silver decorated with frets and borders of green velvet and trimmed with fringes of gold thread and green silk, is also likely to have come from Chatsworth. The eight stools of black and white carsey embroidered with needlework flowers and trimmed with red and black fringe were probably new. Carsey (or kersey) was a widely made twill-woven woollen cloth of varying quality.

Displayed on the window sills, or perhaps across the arms of the chairs, as shown in the portrait of Queen Elizabeth in the Gallery (28), were seven long cushions. Six were of cloth of gold or silver variously decorated with green, black and red velvet, the latter set with silver spangles, and another with a rose 'imboste in the middest'. The seventh was of white satin embroidered with gold twist. All had silk linings and were trimmed with silk and gold fringes and tassels. None has survived. There were two green curtains for the windows, which is rather puzzling since the room has six windows; it has been suggested that the big bay with four windows was cut off to form a separate room, although no such room is mentioned in the inventory. As in the Withdrawing Chamber, there were many portraits on the walls and also a picture of the Virgin and a glass panel painted with the arms of Bess and Lord Shrewsbury.[69]

The Low Great Chamber must have been the scene for a great deal of noisy chatter and various activities, including the playing of cards and board games, sewing and singing. Indeed, the house as a whole would not have been a silent place, despite Bess's increasing age and the problems with Henry and Arbella. Several groups of actors came, including, in August 1600, the Queen's players,[70] and there seems always to have been music. When Bess formally moved into the unfinished house in October 1597, members of the household played for her and various payments are recorded – to the Earl of Rutland's musicians, 'to them that plays of musyke', and 10s was given 'to them that played with Mr. William'.[71] This was not her son William – although, like his brother Charles, he was a patron of music – but her young grandson.

Bess appears to have been well pleased with her new house and, as already noted, the importance that she attached to its furnishings is forcibly expressed in her will. Only a handful of items was given away; her eldest daughter Frances Pierrepont was given the 'greate booke of gould sett with stones with her fathers picture and my picture drawne in yt'; her grandson William Cavendish was left a cup of lapis lazuli to be 'an heirloom to goe with the house of hardwick'; and her daughter Mary Talbot, Countess of Shrewsbury, was given, by a codicil of 1607, the great pearl bed of 1547 with the associated furniture in the room, excluding the wall hangings.[72] This is the only important piece of furniture to leave the house on Bess's death and sadly – given its importance to her – it is likely to have met the same fate as a pearl-embroidered saddle cloth recorded in the 1588 inventory of the Earl of Leicester's effects, with the note, 'all the pearle taken of by my lady'.[73]

Despite Bess's stern admonitions to her descendants, nothing could prevent the gradual decay of almost all her 'household stuffe' in the course of the following centuries, but, before charting that decay, more needs to be said about the most personal of Bess's furnishings: her needlework, embroidery and other stitched pieces.

Chapter Three

EMBROIDERY, NEEDLEWORK AND OTHER TECHNIQUES

The 1601 inventory shows that a high percentage of the textile furnishings in the New Hall were decorated by one or more stitch techniques, but although much survives, more has vanished. There are no beds to show either the richest combinations of materials and techniques or the simple use of woollen cloth stitched with blue, green or white thread; there are no thick wool embroideries, quilted covers, or furnishings trimmed with braid, lace and fringe. None the less, the surviving pieces include types of work unique to Hardwick and a sufficiently wide range of techniques to illustrate those mentioned in the inventory and to reflect the different skills of the people, amateur and professional, whom Bess employed to make her furnishings.

The raw materials were purchased locally at Chesterfield, Derby or at the 'Lenton fayre' in Nottinghamshire. A great deal was sent down from London and some was occasionally bought from abroad, as in 1575 when one of Lord Shrewsbury's ships returned from Rouen with '14 lbs of fine sleyed silk for my lady, being of all colours, at 32s the lb'. This was the smooth floss or untwisted silk that she used in her needlework, for which '3 ells of whited canvas at 3s 5d the ell' were bought at the same time.[1] The necessary working space and equipment were also provided; there was an embroiderer's chamber and inner chamber at the Old Hall and in 'a roome at the wardrop dore' in the New Hall were 'nyne payre of beams for embroders'. These were adjustable embroidery frames (**31**), and the nine pairs no doubt varied in size to take anything from a cushion cover to one of the huge hangings. The fabric was stretched between them and the beams were sometimes called 'tents', from the French *tenter*, to stretch, hence also the name tent stitch. There was a 'short tent' in store at Chatsworth.

The Embroiderers

There is no evidence that Bess herself was a compulsive embroider, but she certainly worked some of the small pieces remaining in the house, probably to while away the time as she sat with Mary Queen of Scots,[2] but her granddaughter Arbella was a skilled needle-woman, as were other of her daughters and granddaughters. Bess's gentlewomen and other servants were certainly involved, but, because they were salaried staff employed for other purposes, their work is not recorded. This was even the case when itinerant professional embroiderers, moving like other craftsmen between the big houses, were taken into the household on a salaried basis and their names, but not their occupation, were entered in the wages lists. There is nothing as clear in the Hardwick accounts as an entry in the records of the Kitson Family of Hengrave Hall, Suffolk, for October 1572: 'Paid the embroiderers for vij weeks and iiij days work in embroydering work at vijd the daye, xxxs viijd.'[3] Bess's comparable use of short-term labour is shown, however, by the payment made in August 1599 to Tasker 'for tarrying three days to make me up ij gownes

30 One of eight panels decorated with strapwork and with heraldry relating to Bess and her family. Cut-pile velvet with appliqué cut from cloths of gold and silver, outlined and linked by silver and silver-gilt thread and cord couched with coloured silks. The initials ES for Elizabeth Shrewsbury are worked in gold twist, other details are in coloured silks. (66 × 52cm) Inv. T/405 *NTPL/John Hammond*

. . . a dublete and a waste cote and doing some other thing',[4] and, although scarce, there are enough specific references to embroiderers to suggest their varying skills and terms of employment.

The accounts for 1548 to 1550, when Bess was dividing her time between London and Northaw, contain several mentions of 'my' and 'the' embroiderer and, although it is not clear whether this was always the same man, it does seem to be the case with the first few entries. They start with the purchase of a substantial quantity of metal thread: one pound in weight of gold and another of silver, each costing £3 6s, more than the annual salary of all but the highest paid of Cavendish's servants. Silk thread was also bought at 16d an ounce (£1 1s 4d per lb), some to couch (hold down) the metal thread and some, of twisted gold and white, to use decoratively. Metal-thread embroidery was highly skilled and when combined with fine wool or silk it was the preserve of the professional male embroiderer. It seems odd, therefore, that some basic tools were also bought, including 'the thynges that the yembrother wyndes hys golde on' (a broach), which cost 16d. A little later, 12d was 'geven to my ymbrother to by hys thymbylles and sheres'. Perhaps he was a journeyman only recently out of his apprenticeship, but he seems to have pleased Cavendish and Bess well enough, since both made him occasional gifts of 4d. He was provided with some clothes, but not a livery coat, and there is one reference to 10s paid to the embroiderer 'in part payment of his quarters wages'. This suggests that, if it was the same man, he had become a member of the household and that he was probably paid 13s 4d a quarter, the same as the porter. There is also a payment of 3s 4d 'to the ymbrother that came from London' (to Northaw) but there is no indication of what he was working on.[5] This is also the case with two other embroiderers, presumably members of the household, who are each mentioned once by name: 'Angell my ymbrother' in 1550 and Barnet in 1552.[6]

There is a long gap before another embroiderer can be identified. This is Thomas Lane, who headed the list of people Bess claimed had been responsible for the hangings of *The Virtues*, made at Chatsworth in the 1570s (see pp.15 and 68). The others were Ambrose, William Barlow, Mr Cavendish's man Henry, and other members of the household, including 'some boys I kept'. None of these can be identified, although it would be nice to think that the Henry of the 1570s was the Henry Travice who, by the 1590s, was running William Cavendish's London house, looking after his affairs and, as already noted, despatching quantities of embroidery silk, braids and other trimmings to Derbyshire (see p.31).

Thomas Lane does not appear in the account books until 1599, but, given the gaps in the books, this is not surprising. Nor is the fact that he worked for Bess over a period of

31 Embroidery frames in a 16th-century woodcut, after Bernard Salomon, of the *Story of Arachne* from Ovid's *Metamorposes*. Having made the mistake of winning a weaving competition against the goddess Minerva, Arachne tried to hang herself but was instead turned into a spider. The work on Minerva's frame, on the left, could be tapestry-woven, but that on Arachne's looks more like needlework.

twenty-five years, as did others of her craftsmen. In December 1599 Lane was paid 40s 'for the tyme he wroughte of the bed and hanging'; that this was for about two months' work is shown by another payment in December 1600, 'to Lane for working towe monthes or x weeks, fortye shellings'. At quite long intervals, he was also paid 'for his work, xls' in June 1600, and 'for his wages, 12s 6d' in March 1601. Despite this last entry, his name never actually appears in the wages lists, so he seems to have been called in only when he was needed.[7]

The hangings on which Thomas Lane had worked in the 1570s included some of velvet decorated with applied canvas-work motifs and at least one set of the great appliqué hangings of *The Virtues*. Although depending on technical skills quite unlike those used in metal-thread work, appliqué – in which separately made motifs were applied to another fabric – was similarly classed as embroidery and was always the work of male professionals. Thomas Lane's skills combined those of embroiderer and upholsterer,[8] and his intermittent work between 1599 and 1601 suggests that he was engaged in mounting fabric or pre-embroidered motifs on large-scale furnishings, perhaps including the hanging for which black velvet was bought in May 1599 (see p.31). As the rooms at the top of the New Hall were the last to be finished, it is possible that Lane was working on the very fine furnishings in the Turret Chamber; the wall hangings were 'imbrodered upon white damask [with] murry velvet and other stuffe', while the bed had vallances 'of black velvet set with stagges and talbottes [hounds] imbrodered with silvines,' and 'Pants [lower valances] to goe about the sides of the bed at the bottome of clothe of golde and crimson velvet'. That the bed was new is indicated by the 'pece of buckerom about the bed to cover it'.

Another embroiderer working in the house in the late 1590s was John Webb; he had been a member of the household at least temporarily since he was paid a half-year's salary of 26s 4d at Midsummer 1598, but he was probably the 'John imbrotherer' who was given 11s 'at his going way' the following February. There is no hint as to what he was working on, nor is there anything to suggest what had been done in February 1598/9 for the substantial sum of 20s 'geuen to ned franke for hys boy to work at Imbradrey upon a reconing'. The family was clearly associated with Hardwick, since, in August 1600, Franke's wife was paid 10s 'for starching some peces of wrought hanging'.[9]

Wrought Linen

The use of starch shows that the hangings were made of linen, and they probably needed starching to regain the crispness lost when they were embroidered. The fine bed in the Turret Chamber had three curtains 'wrought with black silk needlework uppon fine holland Cloth', and there was a second set of tester and four curtains 'of lynnen cloth wrought with silke of divers Coulers' in the Ship Bedchamber. If it was the black set that was starched, it is likely to have been worked with Spanish silk, which was noted for its fast dyes and which cost substantially more than London silk.[10]

The term 'wrought', although applied loosely to any decorated item, had a more precise meaning when applied to stitched objects. It was confined to items of linen stitched with silk, linen or metal threads, a form of work that had come into prominence during the reign of Henry VIII. Seamstresses were responsible for pieces stitched with linen thread, but those worked with silk and metal were produced by the silkwomen, who were importers and dealers in metal threads and raw silk, which they also turned into thread and a variety of braids, fringes and other types of *passementerie*. As decorated linen

32 (*right*) and **33** (*below*) Corner
of a large linen cover worked
with red, blue, green and black
silk mainly in stem, whipped
stem, chain, speckling, knotted
and double-running stitches.
The detail below shows a strawberry outlined in stem stitch
with a diaper filling worked
in stem stitch and knots.
(Corner detail: 135 × 53·5cm;
strawberry: 1·3 × 1cm)
Inv. T/386 *V&A* and *SML*

became increasingly fashionable, this developed into a specialist branch of their work. It
was also practised by skilled amateurs but it was never taken up by the professional male
embroiderers. This is reflected in an entry in Bess's accounts for June 1599: 'payde anne
mylnar for a pece of worke wrought wth cullard sylkes, thurteen shelling and geuen to
her xijd.'[11]

According to the 1601 inventories, there was no decorated linen at either Chatsworth
or the Old Hall and relatively little at the New Hall. In store were two pairs of sheets,
seven single and eight pairs of pillowberes, five cupboard cloths, a single 'fayre quition
[cushion] cloth wrought with gold and silver and red and grene silk', a blackwork napkin
and towel made to match one of the cupboard cloths, and two coverpanes which, like the
towels, were for use at table. The only decorated linen out in the house was that on the
two fine beds mentioned above (p.43), but since not even Bess's bed was described as
having sheets or pillowberes, it is clear that the linen in daily use, whether plain or decorated, was simply not recorded, on the assumption that its life was limited and the inventory was for posterity. With one possible exception, none of the surviving pieces can be
matched with those in the inventory but, since there is no reason to date them later than
1601, they must have been either in use at Hardwick or at Oldcotes, Wingfield Manor or
the London house.

The dozen pieces of wrought linen that remain illustrate five different categories of
work. The largest (2·20 × 1·35m) is the end section of a large coverlet (**32**), worked with
cherry red, bright blue, sage green and some black floss silk in stem, whipped stem, chain,
knotted, speckling and other stitches. The centre is filled with a repeating pattern of

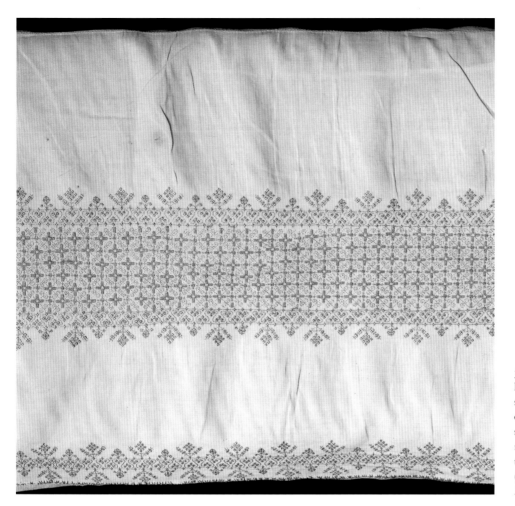

34 Section of a pillow-cover. Fine linen worked with red and green silk (faded) in double-running, cross and two-sided Italian cross stitches. The fineness and regularity of the stitches indicate that this is professional work. (Widest band: 14cm) Inv. T/369 *NTPL/John Hammond*

lobed quatrefoils enclosing sprigs of rose and pink (gillyflower), which touch to form secondary compartments containing formalised sprays of leaves and berries. The continuous border pattern is composed of a series of vases from which sprays of roses, grapes and berries extend outwards to link with a second motif, facing the other way up, of a stylised sprig growing through a square plaque. Different stitch combinations are used to give variety to the berries (33) and clusters of grapes, and all the stitches are worked very tightly and with perfect regularity. This, together with the size of the object, suggests that it is professional work, although not of the finest quality; it was made within the household, perhaps even by Anne Mylnar.

Similar in workmanship and using the same silks, but with a slightly different repertoire of stitches, is a pair of matching but incomplete panels, perhaps originally a towel and coverpane. They are decorated with a border of small leaves and horizontal bands of formalised sprays of flowers, all of which now float in air because the black silk, used to work an enclosing strapwork pattern, has rotted and dropped out. When complete and unfaded, these two objects must have been delightfully fresh and pretty.

A different category of professional work is represented by the remains of two other panels: both were probably pillow covers originally. They are of very fine linen and they have controlled, small-scale repeating patterns meticulously worked in tiny stitches. Bess may have had a very skilled professional working for her, but it is more likely that these pieces were purchased from one of the London silkwomen. The first has a single broad horizontal band filled with latticework containing crosses, which has tiny stiff sprigs extending outwards from its edges (34). They are repeated in the border, where they alternate with small diamond motifs. The pattern is tightly worked with red and green floss silk mainly in double running and cross stitches. The second is worked with red silk, perhaps originally of two shades but now faded to a pinky mauve, in long-armed cross, double running, and two-side Italian cross stitches. The border and one narrow horizontal band contain a single zig-zag line with flattened points surrounded by sprays of oak leaves. To fill the one wide horizontal band, four touching zig-zags were worked to form a series of hexagonal compartments. This piece may be one of the 'payre of pillowberes wrought with red silk' that is listed in the 1601 inventory.

Rather different from the four professional pieces are the remains of a pair of small square cushion covers (35). Their centres are filled with a rather clumsy all-over pattern of wavy lines forming oval, round and ogee compartments that contain ill-defined Ss, rosettes and ovoids. In contrast, the added borders, probably from a different object, are decorated with a deeply looping line enclosing delicate upright sprigs of rose, cornflower, honeysuckle, acorn and other plants. The centre is worked with metal thread and polychrome floss silks, the border only in silk, but the stitches in both – chain, stem, coral, overcast, interlace and speckling – are loosely worked and well within the capabilities of an amateur needlewoman.

Apart from the curtains on the fine bed in the Turret Chamber (see p.43), only five pieces of blackwork are listed in the 1601 inventory, a very small quantity given its popularity, but perhaps Bess preferred a more colourful palette. Among the surviving pieces is a fragment of a small cover worked predominently in black silk, although this is combined with linen thread, tiny cutwork holes and small areas of pulled-fabric work. Sadly, the piece is in very poor condition and almost all the black silk is missing. The stitch holes and the position of the cut holes and open fillings make it possible, however, to re-create its design of bold zig-zag lines crossed by large Ss, with sprigs of acorn within the zig-zags and bunches of grapes hanging between the rows. Although well designed and quite complex in its mix of techniques, this piece is as likely to have been made by a skilled amateur as by a professional embroiderer, as is also the case with the remaining linen items at Hardwick.

These pieces are unique. One is part of a small cover, perhaps a cushion, made of fairly open-weave linen which has been cut and drawn to form a small, net-like grid, which is

35 Part of one of a pair of small square linen cushions, worked with coloured silks and some metal thread in chain, stem, coral, overcast and speckling stitches. (Width: 44cm) Inv. T/392
NTPL/John Hammond

not secured with white linen thread as normal, but is whipped over with cream and pink silk, and patterned with diagonal lines of swastikas outlined by raised knots worked over the intersections of the grid with black silk. A rosette worked in knots of yellow and red silk decorates the centre of each swastika, which is filled with white silk in looped insertion stitches. The background is similarly worked in black silk.

The last four pieces of wrought linen are the most surprising. They form a group of square cushion covers, one complete and three other fragmentary ones. Like the swastika panel, they depend for their effect on pulled-fabric and cut holes, but they are worked on a larger scale and in a geometric format similar to that of white cutwork, the forerunner of needlelace. Instead of following the weave of the linen, however, they are cut on the cross and, in place of linen sewing thread, they too are worked with polychrome floss silks and metal threads (**36**). The complete cover (**37**) is trimmed with a very narrow plaited braid of silver thread, and there are signs that it was backed with coloured silk which would have shown through the holes.

Nothing else remotely like these pieces has survived, but it is possible that the technique was introduced to Bess by Mary Queen of Scots because, among the furnishings left behind her in Scotland, were 'foure uther naipkynnis of holane claith [holland cloth] and cammorage [cambric] sewit with cuttit out werk of gold and silver and divers culloris of silk'.[12] Mary may have worked such pieces herself, since the work, although fiddly, is relatively simple. Her niece, Bess's granddaughter Arbella Stuart, certainly mastered it, because in 1600/1 her New Year's gift to Queen Elizabeth was 'a scarfe or head-veil of lawn cut-worke flourished with silver and silks of sundry colurs', and, according to Lady Stafford, the Queen took 'an especiall likeing to that [gift] of my Lady Arbellas'. It would be interesting to know whether Arbella made a similar gift two years later, because when Sir Henry Brounker was sent to Hardwick in January 1602/3 to investigate the rumours concerning her, he wrote to the Queen, describing how 'I led the Lady Arbella to the other end of the long gallery, where I told her that your Majesty wished her well and gave

36 Detail of coloured cutwork. The areas of uncut linen were covered with stitches but most of the silk has dropped out leaving only the needle holes. (Central diamond: 7 × 7 cm) Inv. T/391 *SML*

37 Cushion of coloured cutwork. Linen worked with coloured silks and a little metal thread in cut and drawn-thread work, with overcast, satin, stem, chain, blanket, back, knot and double-running stitches. Trimmed with a narrow silk and silver braid. The altered corners suggest that it has been cut down. (40 × 47 cm) Inv. T/390 *NTPL/John Hammond*

her thanks for the new year's gift and did graciously accept it and would be glad to know how she did it.'[13] Arbella's work must have been considerably finer than the surviving pieces at Hardwick.

Needlework

Because of its ground fabric, wrought linen was occasionally referred to as 'needlework', a name harking back to a medieval technique in which the linen was entirely hidden by stitches, as on the hoods and orphreys of church vestments. By the sixteenth century the term was more accurately applied to canvas work, where the ground is covered by cross, tent and other stitches. It was a popular technique, used by both men and women and well within the capabilities of amateurs, although they are unlikely to have tackled the huge table carpets, which required a steady application and a uniformity of rhythm and tension. John Webb and Ned Franke's boy were perhaps needleworkers rather than embroiderers.

In 1601 there were about a hundred pieces of needlework in the New Hall, ranging from chair backs and stool covers, cupboard and table carpets, to a bed and set of wall hangings with borders and applied motifs of needlework, but the technique was used most extensively for cushions, for which 'xx yardes of browne cushin canvas at vijd a yarde' were sent down from London in the summer of 1601.[14] The inventory lists 72 cushions made entirely of needlework and 7 of fabric with applied needlework motifs, out of which 10 can be identified among the 13 long cushions remaining in the house. Between them they illustrate a variety of styles, as well as the work of amateurs and different categories of professional embroiderer.

One distinctive pair with matching borders depicts the *Judgement of Solomon* and the *Sacrifice of Isaac* (**38**), but with the Old Testament figures dressed in French Court fashions dating from the late 1570s to the late 1580s. Although more delicate in scale, they are related to a group of larger furnishings – valances and table carpets – which, on the basis of the costume, have been assumed to come from France or the southern Netherlands.[15]

38 Needlework long cushion of the *Sacrifice of Isaac*. Linen canvas worked with wool and silk in tent stitch and a little laid work. When the 6th Duke had the cushion framed like a picture in 1844 he was 'amused by Lady Shrewsbury assisting at the Sacrifice of Isaac.' The onlookers are dressed in the fashions of the French Court. (61·5 × 137cm) Inv. T/227 *NTPL/John Hammond*

There is nothing to suggest how Bess acquired the two cushions, but they are clearly professional work, being beautifully drawn and meticulously worked with silk and wool in tent stitch with a little satin stitch and laid work for the details. Bess's friend, the Earl of Leicester, had owned four 'longe cushions of frenche needleworke', and it is tempting to suggest that Bess bought two of them when his effects were sold to pay his debts;[16] but Leicester died in 1588, and his cushions would have had to have been newly acquired to fit with the most up-to-date of the costume details, notably the huge, tilted ruffs.

The two cushions were in the Gallery in 1601, when they were described as being 'of needlework, silks & crewel'. Crewel was an alternative name for worsted. Only rarely is the inventory more specific about the materials or techniques of needlework, as in the case of a cushion depicting the *Story of Atalanta*, described as being 'of petepoint [*petit point*]' – the French name for tent or half stitch. The only other stitches named are cross and bred stitch, the latter being a form of braid or plait stitch which was perhaps used on another cushion (**39**), 'of needlework grounded white, a pear tree and slips'. The ground is worked with white floss silk in a variant of plait stitch and the motifs are in tent stitch; the fineness and uniformity of the work suggest the hand of a professional.

Another cushion, not identifiable in the inventory, has an apparently simple, reversible pattern of oak leaves pointing diagonally up and down in alternate vertical rows (**40**), but because of the skilful use of colour and the employment of the stitches (cross, long-armed cross, stem, plait, satin and brick) in varying combinations, it is an immensely satisfying object that merits quiet study. The subtle variations of colour and stitch again suggest a professional or a very dedicated amateur.

Different from the pieces above are three more long cushions, all recorded in the inventory, which illustrate the stories of *Europa and the Bull* (**42**), the *Fall of Phaeton* and *Actaeon and Diana*. They are worked to a fairly high stitch count with coloured silks and silver-gilt and silver thread, mainly in tent stitch but with such realistic details as curled silk to represent hair. Each bears a silver and gold monogram ES, for Elizabeth Shrewsbury, and although this is likely to indicate the owner rather than the embroiderer, Bess was clearly closely involved in their production, including the choice of subject-matter.

The designs of only about a quarter of the needlework items were noted by the

39 Needlework long cushion of a *pear tree and slips*. Linen canvas worked with silk, the ground in a form of plait stitch and the motifs in tent stitch. The naturalistic slips are likely to have been taken from a printed herbal. (56 × 125 cm) Inv. T/156 *NTPL/John Hammond*

40 Detail of a needlework long cushion decorated with vertical rows of oak leaves. Worked with silk in long-armed cross, cross, plait, stem, satin, and brick stitches. Increased variety is achieved by changing the direction of the stitches. (Detail: 14 × 12 cm) Inv. T/156 *NTPL/John Hammond*

inventory clerks; they included five stories from the Old Testament, six from classical mythology, a representative selection of Renaissance ornament designs – fretts, knots, billets and antiques or grotesques – and, outnumbering all of them, trees, fruit and flowers, birds and beasts. These were sometimes combined with heraldry, as on a cushion with the arms of Talbot impaling Hardwick, supported by the Talbot hound and the Hardwick stag, and flanked by two branching trees of mixed fruit and flowers (**41**). It is a typically sixteenth-century piece and, like other surviving cushions, reflects the general interests of the day, but when such an object was made within a household, the choice of subject and its translation into a design depended on the taste and knowledge of the initiator of the project, as well as on the availability of a visual source and someone with the skill to transfer it to the fabric ground.

In discussions about Hardwick, reference has often been made to the apparent scarcity of books in the house, which has been taken as proof that Bess of Hardwick was poorly educated, a doer not a thinker. But this ignores the fact that her bedside reading was pretty tough stuff,[17] and that no books at all were recorded in Arbella's room, which she herself, a known scholar, called her 'quondam study chamber', and where she was described reading and working.[18] Bess had established lifelong friendships with clever and cultured people, including Queen Elizabeth and Lady Bacon, a veritable bluestocking, and there is no reason why she should not have been as familiar with translations of classical literature as she was with the Bible. Her enthusiasm for building will have introduced her to the vocabulary of classical architecture and Renaissance ornament design, and she is likely to have owned some illustrated books and possibly even engravings.

The printed sources for several of her needlework and embroidered furnishings have been identified, and these will be dealt with more fully in the catalogue, but mention should be made of Anthony Wells-Cole's work on the engraved sources for many objects and structural details in the two halls at Hardwick. He shows that many images were achieved by the skilful combination of details taken from a number of unrelated sources.[19] John Balechouse is seen as a key figure behind this, and his involvement with the execution as well as the design of some of the textiles is virtually certain. But he was not the only

41 Needlework long cushion with the arms of Talbot impaling Hardwick, with their supporters, the Talbot hound and the Hardwick stag. Worked with silk on fine linen canvas, the centre in tent stitch with details in cross, stem, split and padded stitches; the border in cross stitch with details in tent stitch. (55·5 × 116·5cm) Inv. T/153 *NTPL/John Hammond*

42 (*above*) Needlework long cushion: *Europa and the Bull*. Linen canvas worked with silk and some gold and silver thread in tent stitch with details in split and stem stitches and couched work. The sea monsters and two of Europa's alarmed attendants on the far right are not in the woodcut used as a source. Between the two women is Bess's ES monogram worked in silver and gold thread. (57·5 × 121cm) Inv. T/102 *NTPL/John Hammond*

43 (*left*) The woodcut, after Bernard Salomon, on which the cushion cover of *Europa and the Bull* was based. It was published in Virgilio Solis's Latin version of *Metamorphoses Ovidii*, 1563. *British Library*

person involved, for the stitched textiles were produced over very many years and within a particular environment. They were made at a time when craftsmen, including painters, still formed a close-knit community and the individuals who worked together on houses like Chatsworth and Hardwick shared both skills and knowledge.

A design for a particular object or detail of a building might be drawn out by one craftsman for another, regardless of their respective specialities, and it is not surprising that marked similarities can be found at the New Hall between designs carved in stone and wood, painted and stencilled on flat surfaces, or worked in embroidery and needle-work. The easy acceptance of such interchanges is provided by a casual comment in a letter from Mary Markham to Bess's daughter Mary Talbot; she was, she said, arranging to have a rush mat made and had got the pattern from the painter.[20] It would be interest-ing to know which painter, or other craftsman, drew out the cushion top showing 'the Platt of Chattesworthe House' (see 9), which was in the Gallery at Hardwick in 1601, but is now at Chatsworth. It provides one of the few images of the Tudor house after its enlargement in the 1570s.

Embroiderers, particularly amateurs, were dependent on others for the transfer of their chosen designs to the working linen or canvas, and the underdrawing, which is visible on several of the Hardwick pieces, is of very variable quality, reflecting an input both from skilled workmen like John Balechouse and enthusiastic members of the household. One interesting feature of several pieces for which the engraved source is known is the alteration of clothing by the substitution of contemporary collars, sleeves and other details. This was presumably done on Bess's instructions, and is well illustrated by the Europa cushion (42), which closely follows a woodcut (after Bernard Salomon) in an edition of Ovid's *Metamorphoses*, published by Virgilio Solis in 1563 (43). Europa's wispy draperies have been replaced by a substantial dress, and her attendants have also acquired dresses and embroidered shifts. Given the number of naked and near-naked women displayed in the house, this was clearly not done out of prudery, but to give the story a relevance to modern life, as was also the case with the professional pieces showing the *Judgement of Solomon* and the *Sacrifice of Isaac*.

Long cushion covers, even when framed and hung like pictures, are easily recognised by their size and shape; other surviving pieces are more of a problem. They include nine long narrow panels, which have been described as bed valances, but no needlework bed valances are mentioned in the inventories, and their depth of 28cm is too short, while their combined length, of just under 12m, is too long. They have been cut and rejoined, so it is difficult to determine their original form, but they were perhaps the upper borders of a set of hangings like that recorded in the Little Chamber off the Best Bedchamber (now the Queen of Scots Room), which had 'long borders of stories in needlework'. The

44 Detail of a needlework panel with a crab, the sign of Cancer, from one of a group of nine narrow panels decorated with landscapes and the signs of the Zodiac. Linen canvas worked with coloured silks mainly in cross and tent stitches but with details in stem and other stitches worked regardless of the weave of the ground. (Height: 29.5cm) Inv. T/203g *SML*

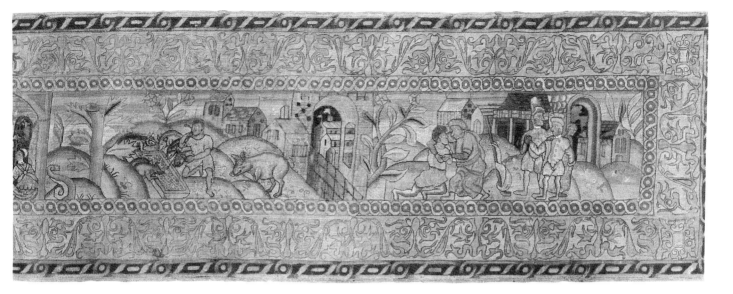

set in question does not tell a story, but shows a continuous landscape with signs of the Zodiac in the sky above. Only nine of the twelve signs are present but, as there are two each of Capricorn and Aquarius, it is possible that there were originally two sets (**44**).

The borders are worked on fairly loosely woven canvas with polychrome floss silks in cross stitch and a few other stitches for decorative details like the stem stitch used for a horse's mane. The underdrawing, which is visible in several places, provides only a simple outline and its naivety is heightened by the angularity of the embroidery and the simplicity of its shading. The panels were drawn out by several people, and the embroiderers, probably Bess's servants, worked side by side, leaving some obvious joins between one person's work and the next. Even in their faded state the panels have the charm of a frieze designed for a child's room; when new, they must have been enchanting.

Rather more sophisticated in intent and execution is another set of narrow panels, two complete and part of a third. They have been described as a set of bed valances and they do have matching borders with the initials ES in the corners, but their subject-matter is unrelated: the story of *The Prodigal Son* (**45**); an unidentified story of a king, shown in a garden, being served with wine, and fighting a wild boar; and in the fragment a personification of Hearing (*Auditus*) as a seated woman playing a lute. If the other senses of Smell, Touch, Sight and Taste were on the missing section, the panel would have been much longer than that showing the Prodigal Son, which it should have matched if from a bed set. It is more likely, as George Digby suggests, that they are cupboard carpets.[21] Four needlework cupboard carpets are listed in the 1601 inventory, two of which are described: one in Arbella's Chamber was 'wrought with antickes and fruit', and the other, in the Best Bedchamber, showed 'the storie of David and Nathan with trees in needleworke and a border of crimson velvet about it & a golde frenge'.

The matching borders of the three surviving panels are similar to the outer border of the largest of the surviving table carpets, which depicts the *Story of Tobit* and is dated 1579. Although the borders of the cupboard carpets are more detailed, they are all in the same flat, outline style reminiscent of inlaid and stencilled patterns on the doors and panelling now in the New Hall. The table carpet and *The Prodigal Son* cupboard carpet are further linked by their pictorial scenes, which are taken from engravings based on illustrations to the Bible by Maarten van Heemskerck. Unlike the simple woodcuts that were enlarged for the *Europa* and other cushions, here fine and detailed engravings had to be drastically simplified, although in both cases the essence of the originals is retained. On

45 Section of a needlework panel (probably a cupboard carpet) depicting the story of *The Prodigal Son*. Linen canvas worked with silk in tent stitch and silver and silver-gilt thread in plaited-braid and chain stitches. One of a group of three panels with matching borders but unrelated subjects; they are twice the depth of the panel shown on a larger scale in fig. **44**. (Height: 57cm) Inv. T/229 *V&A*

46 End border from a needlework table carpet of the *Story of Tobit*, dated 1579. It shows trophies hanging from a balance; on the left, painters' tools and, on the right, embroiderers' – parts of an embroidery frame; scissors and shears; two broachs to hold metal thread; and a unknown object, probably a silk winder. (Height: approx. 57cm) Inv. T/124
NT/John Couzins

the table carpet, the story is told in a series of medallions set in the main border, while the centre contains a large coat of arms of Talbot impaling Hardwick, with their supporters, a coronet above, and below, a tablet with the monogram GES for George and Elizabeth Shrewsbury and the date 1579. The remaining ground is filled with a riot of vegetation, snakes, insects, birds and animals.

An intriguing detail of the design is the inclusion at one end of an elaborate balance, from which hang trophies composed, on the one side, of painters' tools and, on the other, of embroiderers' (46). It would be interesting to know whether Bess had been present a decade earlier, when the newly imprisoned Scottish Queen had 'entered into a pretty disputable comparison between carving, painting, and working with the needle, affirming painting in her opinion for the most commendable quality'.[22] Bess seems to have remained more open-minded or perhaps the question had become a joke between the painter and embroiderer who drew out and worked the carpet.

The Tobit carpet is one of five remaining in the house, but it is not mentioned in the 1601 inventories, nor is the earliest carpet, which is dated 1574 and shows the *Judgement of Paris* (47).[23] The scene is set within a central medallion with a handsome egg and dart frame not unlike some of the Chatsworth moulding later used to frame the long cushions. Surrounding it are large sprays of fruit and flowers and, in the corners, the Hardwick arms alternate with the Hardwick stag. The outer borders, which are also filled with foliage, fruit, birds and animals, are in poor condition and have been turned so that the carpet can serve as a hanging.

Both the table carpets are linked to other needlework pieces by details of their designs, including a distinctive motif of grapes tumbling out from behind a leaf (48). This can also be seen amongst the foliage surrounding the arms of Talbot impaling Hardwick on a third table carpet, which also does not appear in the inventory. Its distinctive feature is a

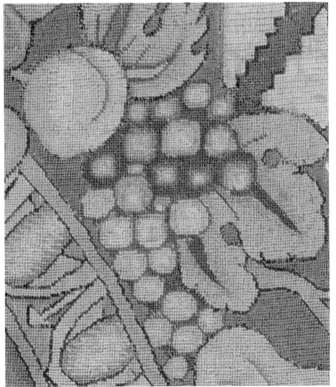

47 (*above*) Needlework table carpet with the *Judgement of Paris*, dated 1574. The Hardwick arms alternate with the Hardwick stag in the centre, and in the borders are the arms of Cavendish impaling Hardwick (top left) and Talbot impaling Hardwick (lower right). Note the initials ES and the grotesque heads on the frame of the central medallion. (115 × 153cm) Inv. T/16
NTPL/John Hammond

48 (*left*) Detail of grapes tumbling from beneath a leaf (from fig. **47**). This motif, worked here with silk in tent stitch, appears on several of the needlework pieces.
NTPL/John Hammond

49 Needlework table carpet with *a rose and antickes*, worked with silk on linen canvas in tent stitch. Originally it had a border of embroidered white satin, trimmed with gold and silver braid and a gold fringe. In 1601 it was in the Best Bedchamber, where it remained until at least the 1760s. (88 × 84cm) Inv. T/463 *NTPL/John Hammond*

single deep border at the top, containing a large house flanked by trees and towers. Although this suggests that it is a hanging rather than a carpet, the coats of arms and badges in the corners are carefully positioned to hang over the edges of a table.

The tumbling grapes also appear on a pair of detached borders, where they are mixed with grotesque images that link them to a fourth table carpet. This one does appear in the inventory, in the Best Bedchamber, where a square table had 'a Carpett for it of nedleworke, made with a rose and antickes' (**49**). The rose is set in the centre of interlaced strapwork that encloses a variety of grotesque heads, animals and insects. Some of these are related to those in two panels showing female herms and also to pieces of needlework later incorporated in one of the hangings of *The Virtues* (see p.72). These links suggest that the whole group was made for the enlarged Chatsworth in the 1570s, and, given their size and number, it is not surprising that sewing silk had to be bought in bulk from abroad. They are all worked with floss silk in cross and tent stitches and are technically within the capabilities of amateur embroiderers. It is only their daunting size, particularly of the Tobit carpet,[24] that suggests that professionals were involved, perhaps including those shut out of Sheffield Lodge by the Earl of Shrewsbury in 1575 (see p.14).

One other surviving table carpet may tentatively be identified as 'one with my Ladies Armes in the middest', which was in the Gallery in 1601. The design of slender branches bearing flowers and pomegranates is quite different from the pieces made in the 1570s,

50 Detail from the centre of a needlework table carpet showing the Hardwick arms below a coronet. The silk thread has dropped out revealing the fine linen-canvas ground and the altered under-drawing. (Height of shield: 50cm) Inv. T/162 *V&A*

and although the Talbot hound alternates with the Hardwick stag in the corners, the use of the Hardwick arms alone suggests that the carpet dates from after the quarrel between Bess and Shrewsbury. Almost all the embroidery silk has dropped out of the shield of arms and the underdrawing shows that it was altered in shape and lengthened before being worked (**50**).

The remaining examples of needlework, several of which were worked by Bess and her gentlewomen, consist of smaller and, in some cases, intriguing pieces. Among the puzzles are two panels (52·5 × 46·5 cm and 51 × 51 cm), which are worked with wool on a fine canvas ground in minute tent stitches, the pull of which has given them a trapezoid shape. They are badly faded and very frail, but their designs are clear. One shows the sun, moon and stars set in a cloudy, wind-blown sky with a rainbow in one corner and an armillary sphere in the centre. The other is roughly divided into quarters representing the four elements: Fire with a salamander at its centre; Water with fish and sea monsters; Earth with flowers and animals; and Air with birds. Coiled in the centre is the Cavendish snake with its motto 'CAVENDO TUTUS'. There is nothing else in the collection quite like them, although many other items demonstrate a similar interest in natural history and astronomy. It is possible that they were square cushion covers, but their purpose is really not clear.

Two panels of a similar size, originally square cushions, are very different in design and technique, being worked on quite coarse canvas largely in cross stitch but with highlights in silver-gilt threads (**51**). A diaper of interlaced stems encloses sprigs of thistle, rose and lily, and applied to the centre and four corners are roundels of much finer linen worked in tent stitch and originally padded. These show scenes from the 1573 edition of Gabriel Faerno's *Fables*; that in the centre of one cushion illustrates two frogs on a well-head

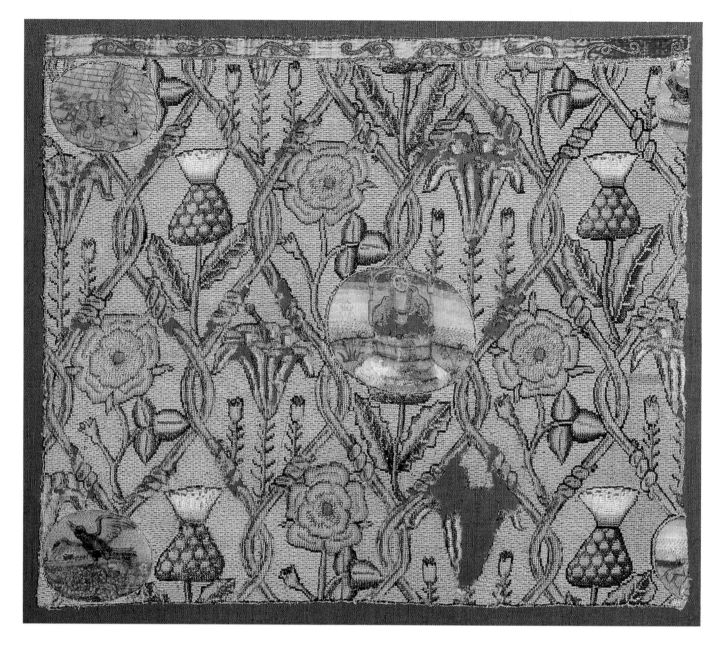

51 (*above*) Panel associated with Mary Queen of Scots. Coarse linen canvas covered with silk and silver-gilt thread in cross stitches worked horizontally, vertically and diagonally, with plaited braid, running and speckling stitches. The applied roundels of finer linen are in tent stitch. (48·5 × 60cm) Inv. T/159 *NTPL/John Hammond*

52 (*right*) Six needlework octagons, all but one initialed ES. Linen canvas worked with silk and wool in cross and some tent stitches. The faded initials and border inscriptions were over-painted by the 6th Duke. (Each octagon: 35·5cm) Inv. F/400 *NTPL/John Hammond*

debating whether or not to jump in, since the well might be dry, and in the background are the crowned initials MAR for Mary Queen of Scots, to whom the thistle of Scotland, the lily of France and the rose of England also refer.

Also linked to Mary are two small cruciform panels (26·5 × 26·5cm) in cross stitch, showing a 'cocle' or hermit crab and a falcon, and thirty-one octagons (38·5cm in diameter) showing plants within borders containing Latin inscriptions (**52**). They match the panels mounted on a set of hangings, now at Oxburgh Hall in Norfolk, which were worked by Bess, the Scottish Queen and their gentlewomen in the 1570s. The octagons remaining at Hardwick, all but two of which bear Bess's initials, show naturalistically drawn flowers, as do six octagons on the two Oxburgh hangings that are associated with her, unlike those on the hanging associated with the Scottish Queen. Also, in place of the pointed mottoes chosen by Mary, the inscriptions on Bess's octagons are Latin tags of the sort learnt by schoolboys – taken perhaps from the old school books of her three sons. John Nevinson has identified the source of the plants as the 1568 and 1572 editions of a book by the botanist Pietro Andrea Mattioli, of which perhaps Mary and Bess each had one copy.[25] Bess was certainly interested in gardens; she had those at Chatsworth and Hardwick laid out well before the houses were finished and her accounts record the

53 Unused slip of a cornflower worked with silk in tent stitch, *c.*1590. Unlike the slips at Hardwick, it has not been cut from the fine linen-canvas ground on which it was worked. (25 × 19cm) *V&A* (T.47–1972)

54 Long cushion of faded carnation-red velvet with applied needlework slips outlined with silver thread. The mistletoe berries in the border are of silver purl (now black). (52 × 110cm) Inv. T/192 *NTPL/John Hammond*

'rewards' she made both to her own gardeners and, when at Court, to those of the Queen. Plants and trees were several times sent down from London and, like many keen gardeners, she seems to have exchanged plants with her friends; in March 1592/3, Sir Francis Willoughby's gardener was rewarded with 5s for bringing something, presumably plants, to Hardwick.[26]

Some gardeners still refer to cuttings as slips, the term used to describe the tent stitch flowers which make up a large proportion of the needlework items at Hardwick. Not all date from Bess's time, since, as we shall see, their production remained a popular pastime throughout England well into the seventeenth century. Reference to their production is again better illustrated by the records of other families, as in a note preserved with eight unused slips (**53**): 'Examined this xvii of Feb [15]96 finding the number according to the content above writtine. Yn all lxxix branchis wrot with the halfe stych in the tent',[27] while the inventory of the effects of Mary, Queen of Scots taken in 1586 lists '52 different flowers in petitpoint drawn from life, of which 32 are uncut'. There were also 124 birds, 16 animals and 52 fish, some cut out ready for mounting. Records dating from before Mary left Scotland show that she had her slips outlined with black stitches before she filled in the colours;[28] Bess's gentlewomen simply followed the drawn outlines.

Although specific projects must have been planned, these records show how the slips could be gradually accumulated until there were enough to decorate some item of furnishing. This more casual approach is suggested by a green velvet cushion at Hardwick, perhaps the one listed in the 1601 inventory. The slips are neatly arranged in three horizontal rows, but, on close inspection, it is clear that they do not all match in style and size, and some incomplete ones have been reused. The same is true of another narrow velvet panel, which is too long for a cushion. It is now green but was originally blue, and its size suggests that it may be the centre of a cupboard carpet, possibly even the one 'of blewe velvett imbrodered with needlework flowers', which was in the present Queen of Scots Room in 1601.

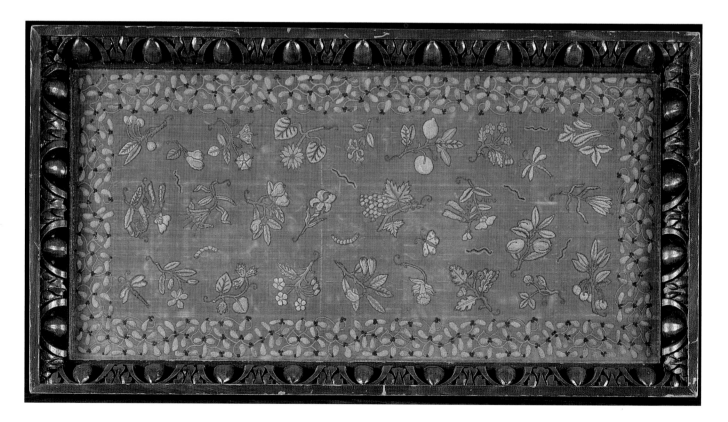

Rather more carefully planned and executed is a cushion of carnation red velvet (now faded to a dull orange) which has a delightful border of mistletoe sprays with stems of couched cord and padded leaves, each with pieces of silver purl for the three tiny berries at its base (**54**). The matching slips in the centre face both up and down and they are outlined with metal thread, which is also used for leaf veins and other details. This was done when the slips were mounted, not only on the red cushion but also on the green and blue pieces, in all cases by a professional embroiderer.

Needlework slips are used on two more long cushions, but here they are combined with much richer materials and, as the clerks noted, mix needlework with embroidery. Both have centres of crimson velvet and one has a border of cloth of silver decorated with applied motifs and the letters E and S cut from red velvet (**58**). In the centre are Bess's arms supported by Hardwick stags and a scatter of needlework slips. The lozenge shape containing the arms shows that Bess was a widow, so the cushion must have been made after Lord Shrewsbury's death in November 1590. The second cushion is decorated with strapwork cut from cloth of silver in the sophisticated style of artists such as Maarten van Heemskerck and Cornelius and Jacob Floris, although some of the fine detail has gone with the loss of the outlining threads (**55** and **56**). The interspaces of the strapwork are filled with naturalistic slips in a typically Hardwick mix of styles.

The last example of needlework on a velvet ground is exceptionally fine. It was described in 1601 as 'one long quition [cushion] the grounde purple velvett, the fancie of a fowler and other personages in needlework', and the other personages have been named as Bess and members of her family, with Bolsover Castle, Derbyshire, in the background (**57**). In reality, the scene is based on one of a set of engravings of hunting scenes after drawings by Joannes Stradanus, which was published by Philips Galle in 1578.[29] The applied motifs are worked with a variety of silk and metal threads, purl and spangles, largely in tent and upright gobelin stitches, and a great variety of textures and realistic effects is achieved by altering the direction of work, by combining the various materials, and by the judicious introduction of other stitches here and there. This is very high-calibre professional work, almost certainly from a London workshop. Hanging from a branch of the tallest tree is a little shield with the initials AC to either side of it. The arms are those of the Keighley family of Yorkshire and, although they are not shown impaled by those

55 (*top*) Long cushion of crimson velvet decorated with applied needlework slips and strapwork cut from cloth of silver. The fine silver threads on the surface of the cloth have tarnished and, in places, broken away to reveal the white silk ground beneath. (53 × 114cm) Inv. T/155 *NTPL/John Hammond*

56 (*above*) Plasterwork overdoor in the lobby of the Paved Room. The 'metallic' strapwork is typical of the many examples at Hardwick worked in stone and plaster and echoed in the velvet cushion (fig. 55). *NT*

57 Long cushion known as the
Fancie of a Fowler. Velvet with
applied needlework motifs
worked with silk and metal
threads combined to rich and
varied rich effect (see fig. **3**).
Closely based on an engraving,
although some costume details
have been changed and one
seated figure on the left has been
turned from a woman into a
man. (52 × 114cm) Inv. T/152
NTPL/John Hammond

of Cavendish, they and the initials must refer to William Cavendish's first wife Anne
Keighley, whom he married in 1582.

Now mounted on nineteenth-century pole-screens (see **99**) are two needlework figures
in the same style as that of the *Fancie of a Fowler* cushion, suggesting that there had been
other pieces of this quality in the house. They were certainly on a par with those objects
accorded the title of embroidery.

Embroidery

Embroidery differed from needlework in its use of rich materials for both the ground and
the decoration, whether this was stitched or applied (**1**). This is well illustrated by two
cushions with red velvet centres and borders of cloth of silver. The one already described
combined the two techniques (**58**); the second is a true embroidery. The crimson centre is
ornamented with rows of the letters E and S, separated by stylised leaves and flowers all
cut from cloth of silver and outlined with blue and yellow silk thread. The border has a
stitched pattern in couched silver-gilt cord.

58 Velvet long cushion with
applied needlework sprigs and
a border of cloth of silver
decorated with applied initials
of velvet and leaves of cloth of
gold, linked by couched metal
threads. The arms are displayed
within a lozenge, indicating
that the cushion was made
after Bess became a widow in
November 1590. Heavily
repaired. (55 × 107cm) Inv. F/398
NTPL/John Hammond

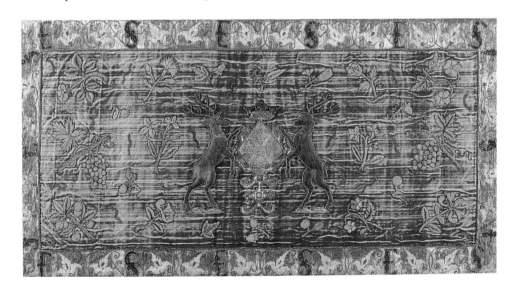

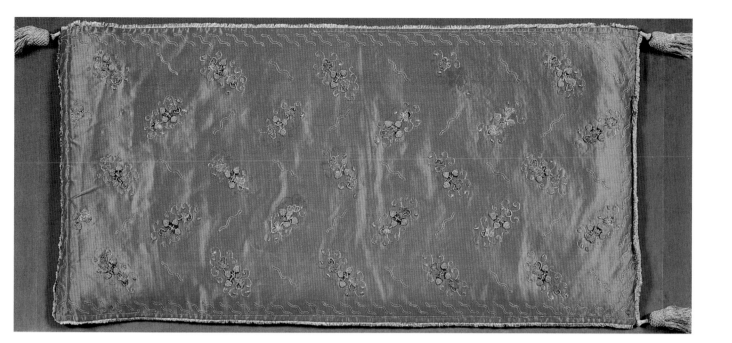

Slightly more complex stitched decoration is shown on the pair of cushions already described as having backs of Chinese damask (see p.29). The fronts are 'of Crimson sattin imbrodered with Straweberries and wormes', worked with black silk and silver-gilt thread mainly in detached buttonhole stitches and laid and couched work on a linen base that also provides slight padding (59). The motifs are outlined and ornamented with couched silver-gilt thread, which is also used for the little worms that slither between the plants and are set diagonally across the narrow border. The motifs tilt alternately to left and right in imitation of a type of pattern found in Italian silks and embroideries of the late sixteenth and early seventeenth centuries, suggesting that the cushions were fairly new in 1601.

Only one example of more complex metal-thread embroidery has survived: a narrow border some 6cm wide and originally more than 7 metres long, although now cut into many short lengths. It is of crimson velvet embroidered with metal thread, strip, purl and spangles in couched work, with slight padding (60). The apparent simplicity of the technique belies the skill involved; this is professional work and the pattern of linked foliate S-shapes is in an international Renaissance style. Narrow borders of this type were called guards, and they were applied to both dress and furnishings, as on the bed in Mr Fortescue's Chamber in the Old Hall, which was 'garded with imbrodered worke of golde twist'. Such embroidery was also used on large objects from chairs to bed sets, although no examples have survived.

The high cost of metal threads meant that they were used sparingly and, because they were fairly stiff and, when twisted together, also bulky, they were seldom pulled through to the back of the fabric. Instead, they were laid on the surface and secured with other

59 One of a pair of unaltered cushions; the tops of satin embroidered with strawberry motifs worked with silver-gilt thread and black silk on linen, and with worms of couched silver-gilt thread. The cushions have their original fringed edging braid, tassels and backs of blue silk damask (see fig. **24**). (56 × 110cm) Inv. T/396 *NTPL/John Hammond*

60 Narrow embroidered guard (or border) of crimson velvet worked with metal purl, twist and spangles; now tarnished but once bright gold and silver. The pattern of linked foliate S-shapes is in an international Renaissance style. (Width: 6cm) Inv. T/290 *SML*

threads, sometimes inconspicuously and sometimes with threads of contrasting colours and textures to create a decorative effect. Padding was used to vary the height of the work and the threads were laid in different directions to create a play of light on the surface, something that was particularly effective in candlelight (**61**). Thick linen and silk threads were also couched rather than stitched, a distinction carefully noted in the inventory; William Cavendish had a bed 'of blue cloth stitched with white thred', while others were 'layde on with twyste of white thred'.

The effect of the latter is illustrated by a group of small panels (30 × 24cm) of blue velvet, now threadbare and darkened almost to black, which are decorated with outline images of armillary spheres, balances, the initials ES and the date 1590 worked with couched silk and metal thread, probably originally white and silver. It is not known how the panels were used, but they were probably incorporated in larger objects such as valances, bedheads or even hangings. Similar pieces are used on the outer columns of the *Faith and Mahomet* hanging (see p.73).

All the other embroidery at Hardwick is in the form of appliqué and includes a group

61 (*above*) Detail from one of a set of small heraldic panels; part of the initials HP for Henry Pierrepont, husband of Bess's eldest daughter Frances. Velvet embroidered with silver purl and thread, gold thread and twist, red silk and metal ornaments. The padding of linen threads is visible where some purl is missing. (Detail: approx. 13·5 × 7·5cm) Inv. T/419 *SML*

62 (*right*) Grotesque motifs cut from velvet, satin and some patterned silks, outlined and decorated with silk and metal thread, cord and with painted details. (Largest motif: 22cm high) Inv. T/295 *NTPL/John Hammond*

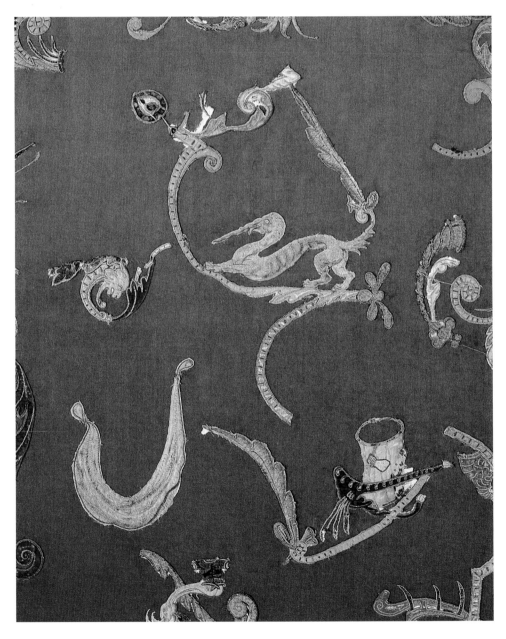

of motifs in the grotesque style, cut from brightly coloured satins and with details worked with silk and metal threads (**62**). The quality of the drawing and the workmanship indicates a professional source, but whether in England or abroad is not clear. Such pieces were made for an international market and could have come from France, Italy or Flanders; they would have been available in London, but Mary Queen of Scots is another possible source.[30]

The remaining appliqué, which was created by professional embroiderers working within Bess's household, falls into three distinct groups, although they all contributed to a single decorative scheme (see p.73). The first group consists of the remains of eight large and twenty-eight small panels of crimson velvet decorated with heraldic motifs set within applied strapwork of cloth of silver. On the large panels (**30**), the strapwork is laid flat and is entwined with trails of applied flowers and leaves (**63**); on the small panels, it is laid over padding in a complex shape composed of a roundel with four trefoils projecting from it (**64**). Extending into the corners between them are four stiff floral sprigs, which, like the flowers on the large panels, are cut from exceedingly rich woven fabrics and are further ornamented with couched silks and metal threads, spangles, metal ornaments and bits of purl. The small panels bear coats of arms, crests and initials relating to Bess, three of her husbands and four of her children and their husbands or wives. Her favourite son William, and Charles, the youngest, are not represented.

The second group consists of eight large panels and forty-eight small ones which match the sizes of the first group, although they are differently decorated. The large

63 (*above*) Detail of one of the large heraldic panels (see fig. **30**) showing the flat strapwork of cloth of silver and applied flowers cut from cloths of gold and silver. The appliqué is outlined with gold and silver threads couched with coloured silks; some details are embroidered with silk. (Detail: approx. 18 × 10cm) Inv. T/366 *SML*

64 (*left*) Small heraldic panel with the Hardwick stag and the monogram ES. Velvet with applied strapwork of cloth of silver laid over padding, and floral sprigs cut from rich fabrics, padded and ornamented with silk and metal threads and cords in couched work and some stitched details. (30 × 30cm) Inv. T/418 *NTPL/John Hammond*

panels depict personifications of the Liberal Arts (**65**); these usually numbered seven, but
here there are eight: Grammar, Logic, Rhetoric, Arithmetic, Astrology, Music and,
instead of Geometry, Perspective and Architecture. The figures are beautifully drawn in
pseudo-classical dress and they stand within arches or portals, which were originally
shown in full perspective. Sadly, the effect is largely lost because they have been cut down
at the sides and the inner profiles of the arches remain only on three, otherwise badly
damaged panels. The details of the pillars and the shading of the recessed panels in the
spandrels show, however, that half were drawn from the left and half from the right,
indicating that they were designed as part of a larger composition.

The arches are cut from cloth of gold with inset panels of blue (faded to green) velvet
ornamented with candelabrum and scrolling stem patterns in couched metal thread,
spangles and metal ornaments. The names of the figures are embroidered on the entabla-
tures, and the keystones are decorated with grotesque animal masks of needlework. The
figures themselves are built up on a linen base, the flesh parts covered with plain silk and
the features and other details embroidered with silk in stem and back stitches, and
delicately shaded with paint (though in many cases the original delicate work has been
crudely painted over). Some painted shadows are also used to define the drapery of the
figures (**66**), which is cut from cloth of silver, striped and stamped taffeta, and other
patterned silks, laid over soft padding, moulded to increase the naturalistic effects. They
stand on chequered pavements of red and white velvet, but the original background of
black velvet has been replaced in all but three panels.

The forty-eight small panels also depict personifications, including Virtues and Vices;
the Sun, Moon, Earth, Water and nymphs of the natural world; Smell from the five
senses; nymphs, gods and goddesses from classical mythology, as well as more abstract
concepts such as Fortune, Abundance and Intelligence (**67**). The figures stand within

68 Lucretia, one of the five appliqué hangings showing famous women of the Ancient World. She was the wife of a Roman nobleman who, after being raped by Tarquinius Superbus, killed herself rather than bring shame on her family. She is shown between the personifications of her virtues – Chastity on the left and Liberality to the right. (277 × 340cm) Inv. T/231b *NTPL*

arches of three different types, one of which matches those of the Liberal Arts panels. The other two are reused arches from ecclesiastical vestments which have been cut in half and widened with inset pieces decorated with grotesque masks in needlework. Like the personifications of the Liberal Arts, these figures are beautifully made from very rich materials, but the panels have been considerably altered and there is a great deal of clumsy overpainting; it is no longer possible to work out the composition of the three groups. The panels, including several empty arches, have been mounted in two huge folding screens; other fragments remain in store.

The third group of appliqué comprises the large wall hangings now mounted behind glass in the Hall and on the Chapel Landing, and now known collectively as *The Virtues* (**68**). They form two distinct sets, depicting between them the three theological virtues of Faith, Hope and Charity, and the four cardinal virtues of Justice, Prudence, Fortitude and Temperance, together with several minor virtues. The subject-matter is not surprising since the Virtues and their contrary Vices had been the stock-in-trade of poets, philosophers and craftsmen working in every medium from classical times onwards, although their personifications changed. In the sixteenth century, under the influence of the Renaissance and the Reformation, the saints of the medieval period were replaced by figures taken from the Old Testament or, as in Bess's hangings, from classical sources, and there was plenty of information on which to draw. The legend of Lucretia, for example, in the version written in 1479 by Aeneas Silvius Piccolomini (later Pope Pius II), was one of the most widely read stories of the Renaissance, and Bess was sufficiently familiar with it to have her last child christened Lucretia in 1557.[31]

Lucretia features on the larger of the two sets, which depicts famous women of the Ancient World each flanked by two personifications of her virtues. There were originally five hangings, showing Lucretia with Chastity and Liberality (**68**), Penelope (**26**) with Patience and Perseverance, Cleopatra with Fortitude and Justice, Zenobia (**2**) with Magnanimity and Prudence, and Artemisia with Constancy and Pietas (the Roman form of filial piety or charity). It is not surprising that the independent and energetic Bess was attracted to a group of noble women, several of whom were rulers in their own right, although the theme of the set is not only power but the women's constancy and devotion to their partners. This is most graphically expressed by Artemisia, the sister and wife of King Mausolus of Caria in Asia Minor. On his death in 353 BC, she not only built the great memorial, or Mausoleum, at Halicarnasus (now Bodrum), but dissolved his ashes in liquid, which she then drank to provide him with a living tomb. She is depicted holding aloft the goblet (**97**).

The second set had only three pieces, each illustrating a virtue and its opposite vice: the contrary of Christian Faith is Mahomet; Hope is contrasted by Judas, the ultimate example of Despair; and in place of Charity, the third theological virtue, Temperance (**71**), is opposed by Sardanapalus, the personification of intemperate indulgence, whose palace was burnt around him as he feasted (**70**). Bess's second child, who died at about eighteen months, was called Temperance, and it does seem to have been a virtue she believed in. The extravagance that led to debt and even bankruptcy was not for her.

These two sets of hangings, which are the most important textiles in the house, are now unique and were rare even in Bess's day. In their size they look back to the large-scale appliqué, then called cutwork, used in the first half of the sixteenth century to make objects such as tents, horse trappings and scenery for pageants, as well as beds and wall hangings. On her earliest visits to Court, Bess may well have seen at Nonsuch in Surrey a set of hangings of red Turkey silk 'enbrodered with horsemen and other images', each of which was some fourteen feet square. The set was described as old in 1547, and more typical of later sixteenth-century appliqué was a second set at Nonsuch, of seven hangings 'of yellow and white satten enbraudered with antiques of the same stuffe with thistorie of the vii workes of mercye imbraudered with silke upon them'.[32] These would have been on a smaller scale, with the works of mercy embroidered within small medallions framed by grotesque decoration. In creating her great hangings Bess seems to have been harking back to the older Nonsuch set and to an ideal of magnificence absorbed in early adulthood, but in the details of their design, she shows a keen awareness of contemporary taste.

There are, however, marked differences between the two Hardwick sets, which can be explained only by considering when and why they were made, and for this it is necessary to go back to the early 1570s and what must have felt like the crowning period of Bess's life. She had increasing wealth, high social status and friends within the highest Court circles, for whom she created the new State Apartments at Chatsworth. The first stage was presumably completed by 1573, when Lord Burghley, in a letter to Lord Shrewsbury, asked to be remembered to his wife, 'wishing myself with her at Chatsworth, where I think I should se gret alteration to my good likyng'.[33] The hanging of Artemisia is dated 1573, but whether this commemorates the completion of the single hanging or of the set of five is unclear. Certainly, work on the house continued in fits and starts throughout the

1570s, with another burst of activity before the visit of Robert Dudley, Earl of Leicester in 1577, when much of the elaborate panelling was installed, although not in the rooms to which he gave his name.

Bess had known Leicester since his youth, when his parents formed part of the social group in which she had moved as Lady Cavendish. Now she enjoyed his hospitality, staying at Leicester House during a London visit in 1576 and in his rooms at Richmond Palace when she attended Court there in 1578. They shared an interest in architecture and Bess borrowed one of his plasterers from Kenilworth; in 1601 one of the books by her bedside, which was dedicated to him, may have been his gift. They are more than likely to have discussed the decoration and furnishing of her new rooms, although *The Virtues* seem unlikely candidates for his rooms, which were probably hung with her best tapestries, perhaps the 'eight rich hangings' bought from Sir William Pickering (see p.15).

The other set of named rooms at Chatsworth were those of Mary Queen of Scots. One was left unpanelled, but the devoted wives of the first set of hangings would seem to be an inappropriate choice for the Scottish Queen. No doubt, she preferred tapestry or, perhaps, the velvet hangings with applied needlework to which Lord Shrewsbury laid claim, and which sound more like the surviving embroideries attributed to her (see p.15).[34] Mary may none the less have been instrumental in starting Bess on the project. In his much quoted letter of 13 March 1569, Lord Shrewsbury described how the Scottish Queen 'daily resorts to my wife's chamber, where with the Lady Leviston and Mistress Seton, she sits devising works', and in September 1570 Mary herself recorded how Bastian Pagez, a gentleman of her Chamber, 'in this dreary time cheers me by the works he invents, after my books, the only exercise that is left me'.[35] There was a portrait of Bastian in the Wardrobe at the New Hall in 1601, and Bess may have made use of his talents in the 1570s, while she and the Scottish Queen were still on good terms and spending much time together. Beds made in matching sets with chairs and cushions had existed at Chatsworth since the 1550s, and the availability of a good designer and, in either Bess's or Mary's service, a skilled embroiderer/upholsterer, enabled her to add large-scale, purpose-made hangings to her decorative schemes. It may not have been purely for frugal reasons that despite her very real wealth, she never commissioned tapestries like Lord Leicester and her other friends; she preferred to keep things under her own control.

In her rebuttal of Lord Shrewsbury's claims in 1586, Bess had argued that the hangings had been made from vestments acquired by her third husband Sir William St Loe, and this is supported by the type of materials used in the first set of *Virtue* hangings and by the survival at Hardwick of hoods and orphreys from dismantled copes (**69**). Some of the same materials were used in the red velvet appliqué panels with heraldry relating to her children's marriages. The absence of William and Charles Cavendish dates them to between November 1574, when Bess's daughter Elizabeth married Charles Stuart, Earl of Lennox, and 1581, when Charles Cavendish married his first wife Margaret Kitson. William married Anne Keighley the following year.

The close relation in size and materials of the above set and the Liberal Arts panels and the small panels with matching arches indicate that these were also made for Chatsworth in the later 1570s. The second set of *Virtues*, however, cannot be so securely tied in, despite the fact that Anthony Wells-Cole has identified the figures of the Vices as being taken from a set of engravings by Hans Collaet the elder, one of which is dated 1576.[36] Apart from slight alterations to their clothing, the half-figures are reproduced in precise detail, but instead of standing behind a high platform on which the Virtues are seated, as in the engravings, they rise strangely from the floor at their feet. The Virtues themselves bear no resemblance to those of the engravings, being, like the famous women of the

69 Remains of late 15th- and early 16th-century vestments: the background is a patterned cloth of gold with raised loops (a tissue); on it are pieces from orphreys – a fragment of a figure within a gothic arch and half an arch matching some used in the small panels with personifications; a slip of patterned silks from a cope 'powdered' with similar motifs; and a piece of embroidered braid from the hem of a cope. A matching tissue panel is used for the skirt of Faith in one of the appliqué hangings. (Tissue ground: approx. 55 × 80cm)
Inv. T/256, 308, 381, 294, 379
NTPL/John Hammond

70 (*left*) and **71** (*right*) Details of the hanging of *Temperance and Sardanapulus* from the second *Virtues* set. The burning palace is taken from an engraving of 1576 but the standing figures are based on sources ranging in date from the 1560s to the late 1590s. The pilasters that frame the scene and separate it from the figure of Temperance are made from fragments of a needlework panel *c.*1570. Note the beautifully drawn table. (Palace scene: 136 × 84cm; Figure of Temperance: 137·5cm) Inv. 232b *NTPL/John Hammond* and *Anthony Wells-Cole/Robert Thrift*

first set, rather stiff figures owing much to contemporary English portraiture. Similarly, only a few details of the background are echoed in the embroidery, most clearly the burning palace of Sardanapalus (**70**), but even here the figures have been clothed in sixteenth-century European dress. Even more strange is the conversion of the mosque behind Mahomet into a Christian Gothic church, but with figures in Turkish dress taken from yet other engravings.

The sources for the alternative images have not been found, but details of the European costume indicate that they varied in date from the late 1560s to the mid- to late 1590s, making it impossible for them to have been completed at Chatsworth before Bess left for Hardwick in 1584. The set cannot, therefore, have formed part of the disputed hangings over which Bess and her husband quarrelled. This suggests that although the set was planned at Chatsworth, almost certainly to have more than three pieces, it was completed at Hardwick. With the exception of the fabrics used for the skirts of the *Virtues*, this set lacks the rich materials used for the famous women of the first set and, as already mentioned (p.70), one hanging, Temperance (**71**), incorporates reused pieces of needlework, apparently taken from large furnishings contemporary with the Tobit table carpet.

On the Faith hanging, small panels of velvet decorated with couched metal thread in the same technique and incorporating one of the same motifs used on the dated blue velvet panels discussed above (see p.64), suggest a date for their completion in the 1590s.

Without room sizes or an inventory, it is impossible to say where the first set of *Virtues* and the related panels hung at Chatsworth, but the Low Great Chamber was probably the most likely of the unpanelled rooms. At Hardwick, however, the 1601 inventory describes a unified scheme, based on personifications set within classical arches, spread across the Withdrawing Chamber, the Best Bedchamber and the passage that linked it to the Gallery. The three hangings of the *Virtues* and their contrary *Vices*, and probably some of the small personifications, must have been completed to fit this scheme, although, to fill the space, it was necessary to use the four hangings of green velvet with applied needlework, which had been made for Chatsworth before 1584. The best bed was described as having a 'sparver and bedeshead with double vallans of cloth of gold, cloth of silver and sondry Coulers of velvet embroidered fayre with divers arms with portalls and pictures', while, in the corridor were nine hangings 'of white cloth with pedestalls and portalls of other coulers and . . . with portalls and pavements rounde about'.

The remains of this glory was recognisably described by Horace Walpole in 1760, although the coverlet of the Best Bed was 'all in tatters of cloth of gold and silver paned, with pieces of different patchwork and embroidery', and he confirmed that 'on this bed are arms of several Earls and Countesses'.[37] The fact that the small heraldic panels were mixed with the small personifications on the bed is supported by a drawing of 1785 by S. H. Grimm (**72**), in which the valances and possibly the headcloth are shown mounted on a modern white bed in the Queen of Scots Room. The small panels with roundels, trefoils and stiff sprigs are clearly visible, together with arches containing figures. Other of the large and small panels must have decorated the hangings in the passage.

Given the superb quality of their materials and the accomplishment of their design and execution, it is not surprising that these spectacular furnishings were respected and preserved despite the inevitable damage wrought by time.

72 Drawing made in 1785 by S. H. Grimm of a bed in the Queen of Scots room at Hardwick. The valance is composed of small heraldic panels alternating with small personifications; a second length is mounted at the top of the headcloth, which is made-up with further fragments from the Best Bed and associated hangings.

Stained Work

In the late fifteenth and early sixteenth centuries, when many smaller craft guilds were combined, the stainers joined together with the painters and members of the resulting Painters' and Stainers' Guild worked in a variety of techniques on textile-based objects ranging from tents and horse-trappings to the costume and scenery for pageants and tournaments, as well as such domestic items as wall hangings. Very little of their work has survived, but it is represented in one of the most interesting groups of textiles at Hardwick: one that combines painting and embroidery.

John Balechouse, who was also known as John Painter, turned his hand to many forms of work, including wall painting, probably panel painting, and stencilling.[38] He was responsible for the painted hangings now in the Chapel at Hardwick, which must have been completed after 1601 since they do not appear in the inventory, and also for stained hangings. On 8 February 1599/1600 'paynting stuff [was bought] for John Painter for staying the cloth hanging', which may have been one of a set of eight made for alternative use in the High Great Chamber;[39] it was of 'woollen cloth stayned with a frett and storie and silk flowers'. The silk flowers would have been cut from fabric and applied by the embroiderers, perhaps Thomas Lane and his assistants, including one called Amyas, for whom dye stuff had been bought in 1595.[40] In the Gallery Chamber was a more simple cupboard carpet of 'saye stained red and white', and in the Wardrobe was a canopy 'of yellowe saye stayned with birdes and Antickes'.

The pieces of stained saye have not survived, but both a fret and birds feature on a set of panels still at Hardwick. The set consists of nine panels, each measuring 68·5 × 69·5cm, and made not of saye, but of velvet (**73**). Each panel is composed of nine cruciform shapes of blue velvet, now faded to a dull green. The cruciforms have concave

73 One of a set of nine panels made from blue velvet (now green) with inset roundels of white velvet. The strapwork is stained a darker colour and outlined with couched bundles of silk thread. The birds and other motifs are stained in several coloured (now faded) and details are stitched with silk. (68·5 × 69·5cm) Inv. T/462
NTPL / John Hammond

sides and, consequently, leave four round spaces in the centre of each panel and eight semi-circles and four quadrants round the edges. These spaces are filled with white velvet outlined with bundles of loosely twisted yellow (now cream) silk thread. The blue velvet is marked out with a fretwork of narrow lines stained a darker colour than the ground and outlined with yellow silk twist. The four white velvet roundels on each panel are decorated with birds drawn from a repertoire of seventeen different images; lively and distinctive though they are, their source has not yet been identified. In the corner quadrants are snakes, lizards, frogs, lobsters, snails, beetles, dragonflies, butterflies, grasshoppers and other insects, while the semicircles contain flowers, fruit and nuts.

The motifs were drawn on the white velvet and stained, apparently with different colours including green and red, but they have all faded to shades of brown. The motifs are outlined with black silk in stem stitch, green silk is used to work the veins of the leaves and the eyes of the birds and other details were also embroidered. Some of these have been overpainted during later repairs. The motifs round the edges have been carefully adapted to fit the confined space, showing that the panels were not intended to be joined edge-to-edge, but probably to be paned with intermediate bands of plain fabric. If all nine were arranged, with panes, in a single block, the resulting hanging would have been very large and somewhat at odds with its small-scale and delicate decoration, but it is not easy to suggest a more satisfactory use.

This would also seem to be a problem with another group of stained objects: twenty-three small oblongs (20 × 14cm) of green, now beige, velvet stained in a darker shade with a symmetrical design, outlined in couched silk twist, of stylised leaves extending from a small central roundel. A clue to their purpose is provided, however, by the hanging of *Faith and Mahomet*, in which both the floor and the columns at either side are put together from small rectangular panels with simple patterns of stained work outlined with cord. The two hangings of *Faith* and *Temperance* have been repaired several times and there is a great deal of overpainting, but the stored remains of the third hanging, of *Hope and Judas*, show that painting and staining were used extensively in this second set of the *Virtues* and the oblong panels were probably used as building-blocks within it.

As already indicated, colour wash was also used to shade the faces and clothing on the Liberal Arts panels and the associated small personifications, as well as on the red velvet heraldic panels. There is also a small fragment of painted satin combined with a fretwork of green velvet in the Victoria and Albert Museum (**74**), which was discovered serving as a patch behind a panel on the Oxburgh hangings. It fits rather well with a description in the 1601 inventory of a form in the Gallery that was 'Covered with grene velvet and white sattin stayned'.

There is more information still to be teased out of the Hardwick records, but those for the late 1590s and early 1600s suggest a final burst of creative energy, as Bess's workmen, and in particular her painters and embroiderers, completed the interior decoration of the New Hall.

74 Fragment from a valance or border of linen covered with white satin stained (painted) with birds and other motifs, and applied strapwork of green velvet edged with bundles of silk thread. (26·5 × 11cm) *V&A (T.33LL–1955)*

Chapter Four

THE SEVENTEENTH AND EIGHTEENTH CENTURIES

Bess's second son William Cavendish was in his fifty-seventh year when he inherited Hardwick in February 1607/8, and on 10 April of the same year his eighteen-year-old heir, also William Cavendish, was reluctantly married to the twelve-year-old Christian Bruce, heiress to Edward Bruce, Lord Kinloss, a favourite of King James I. It was a marriage that was to affect the fortunes of the family for much of the seventeenth century.

William Cavendish the elder had been created 1st Baron Cavendish in 1605, thanks to the influence of his niece, Arbella. He was a shrewd business man, active in various overseas companies, including the newly formed East India Company.[1] When in London he lived at his house in Aldersgate and, although an unwilling courtier, he also attended Court, for he was well aware of the importance of rank and no doubt considered the £10,000 that ensured his creation as 1st Earl of Devonshire in 1618 as money well spent. Having long assisted his mother in the running of her estates, he continued their prudent management after her death, and in 1608 he bought the house at Chatsworth for £8,000 from his elder brother Henry. William seems to have abandoned Oldcotes and to have divided his time between London, Chatsworth, which he presumably refurnished, and Hardwick, where he spent the considerable sum of £1,163 5s 6d in work on the New Hall and a substantial addition to the Old. It would be interesting to know whether he had been itching to carry out his own schemes or whether he was completing projects long planned by Bess.[2]

A large account book for the years 1608–22 provides a detailed picture of William's day-to-day expenditure, although, as in his mother's accounts, distinctions are seldom made between fabric bought for furnishings and that for dress, nor is there information about the intended location of such objects as the 'dozen stooles couered wth hally fax [Halifax] cushions', bought in October 1609.[3] The relative amounts spent in various areas is suggested, however, by a 'Briefe of all Disbursmts' made during the year from Michaelmas 1622 to 1623. He spent £848 1s 5d on arras (tapestry) for his households at London, Lattimers (in Buckinghamshire), Chelsea and Derbyshire, while, of the fourteen tradesmen listed, the bills of the linen draper totalled £16 16s, those of the woollen draper £37 17s 6d and of the mercer £63 1s. By comparison, he spent £19 17s with the goldsmith and a total of £40 10s with the coachmaker and harnessmaker. The wages of all his servants totalled £278 17s 8d for the year.[4]

The best indication of William's personal taste is provided by an inventory taken in 1617 of his London house in Aldersgate, a substantial building of some forty-five rooms.[5] The descriptions are brief, but the house was well furnished with matching upholstery in the principal rooms: 'All of blue velvet wth blue silk fringe' in the Gallery, crimson velvet trimmed with red silk braid and fringe in the Withdrawing Chamber, and turkey-work in the 'Wainscot Room'. There were separate suites, including closets, for him and Lady Cavendish. Her bed was hung with blue damask, laced and fringed in yellow and blue,

75 Canopy and associated chairs in the High Great Chamber made for Christian Bruce, wife of the 2nd Earl, whose arms (of Cavendish impaling Bruce) are in the centre of the backcloth. The canopy has been extensively altered, first by the 6th Duke and then by the Duchess Evelyn; it now incorporates both 19th and 20th century additions as well as motifs dating from Bess's time. Canopy: Inv. F/513; chairs: F/362 *NTPL/Nadia MacKenzie*

76 Christian Bruce (1595–1675), wife of the 2nd Earl; detail from a group portrait painted in the late 1620s. Her accounts show that she was responsible for having many new furnishings made for Hardwick and other Cavendish houses. *Devonshire Collection*

and with a green silk quilt. His was entirely fitted out in crimson taffeta trimmed with silk fringes and he had a great chair with elbows and two high stools 'All of stamell [a type of worsted] laced and fringed wth crimson and yellow'. With the exception of the panelled room, the walls were hung with tapestries of unspecified type, and there were many Turkish carpets on the floors as well as on the tables and cupboards – the product perhaps of his own trading ventures. Like his mother, William clearly believed in having 'that which is needful and necessary' to his rank.

The 1st Earl of Devonshire died on 3 March 1625/6 and was succeeded by his son William, a very different character. He was no fool, being a good linguist and, with the mathematician and philosopher Thomas Hobbes as his tutor and companion on his travels abroad, not uneducated. But he was wildly extravagant, running up enormous debts in anticipation of his inheritance, and continuing with equal irresponsibility after his father's death. Rather than look after his estates in Derbyshire and elsewhere, he preferred life in London, perfecting the accomplishments of the courtier, including the art of dress, as his portrait at Hardwick shows. His taste in furnishings was no doubt as luxurious, but there is nothing at Hardwick that can, with certainty, be attributed to his brief period as its owner. He died at his London house in 1628, only two years after his father; he was thirty-eight years old.

His heir, yet another William, was only eleven at the time, and responsibility for dealing with the debts that encumbered his estate fell upon his mother, Christian Bruce (**76**), who was by then thirty-two years old, with three young children. She was eulogised by Thomas Pomfret as one whose conversation was noted for its 'Delicacies of Expression and Harmony of Reason', but in addition she had the qualities of 'Prudence, Dilligence, Resolution and Bravery', which, with a mix of frugality and wise spending rivalling that of Bess, enabled her to put the family finances back on a firm footing. She was successful to the extent that 'both by her own Prince, and strangers, [she] was Reputed to live greater than any subject whatsoever, as to Hospitality, Resort and Retinue.'[6]

It was Christian Bruce who installed the canopies of state in the High Great Chamber (**75**) and Gallery at Hardwick, and who also owned the bed of blue silk damask (**77**) decorated with applied needlework motifs, now remounted on the bed in the Blue Room (see **83**). It is dated 1629, which was the year after her husband's death. According to Thomas Pomfret, 'every day, after she had first Accounted to God for herself, she then took the Accounts, even to the minutest Expences, of what the preceding Day had consumed'.[7] Most of these detailed accounts have vanished, but one book, dealing with household expenditure for the years 1635–7, provides an illuminating picture of a period when the finances of the estate were again under control and the political affairs of the nation not yet in disarray.[8]

In the half year from Lady Day (25 March) to Michaelmas (29 September) 1635, for example, £1,947 17s 8d was 'paid and disbursed for the use of the right hon' Christian, Countess Dowager of Devonshire', of which £183 7s 7d represented the half-yearly wages of forty-five members of the household – a figure that is worth bearing in mind when considering the cost of the textile furnishings. The family's main houses were at London, Leicester Abbey, Chatsworth and Hardwick, and the expenditure on them was recorded under various heads, including 'Buildings and Repairs', 'Church and Parish Duties', and 'Necessaries', which covered various things from paper, corks and bottles to damask powder and cedar wood 'to sweeten the lynen' and protect against moth. By far the largest outlay was on the stables and travel; it was at least three times the expenditure on 'Diet and Housekeeping', and six or more times the sums spent on 'Household Stuff'.

This last heading covered items as diverse as 'a lyne for the Laundrie, 8d' and £412 for

77 Detail of a bed valance of blue silk damask decorated with applied needlework motifs and trimmed with a fringed braid of white, yellow and blue silk. The damask ground has a pattern of large curving sprigs which date it to *c.*1625–50; it is quite unlike the replacement damask woven for the blue bed in 1852 (fig. **83**) and supposedly copied from the original. (Depth: 27·5cm) Inv. T/70a *NTPL/John Hammond*

'8 peeces of hangings'. Neither the type of hangings nor the house for which they were intended is noted, although this information is sometimes given. In late March 1635, for example, '25 ells of black and white taffetie at 7s per yard' (a total of £8 15s) were bought 'To line the bla' bed at Hardwk', and a few days later, '8 dozen of black and white lace' costing £1 15s 6d was also bought for hangings at Hardwick, presumably for the same bed.[9] Early in September 1635, £1 4s 2d was paid for '4 dozen of Black Statute Lace for the lowe drawing roome at Hardwick', but there is no indication what it was for, nor are there further details about the 'tauny velluet suit at Hardwick' for which Henry Kersie supplied '4 oz of working gold at 5s 6d thoz and 2 oz of silver at 5s p. oz': a total of £1 12s.

Henry Kersie was a silkman or haberdasher whose name appears frequently, as does that of Stephen Collins. He was an upholsterer who supplied yardage fabrics, like the 41 yards of yellow bays costing £3 15s 2d which was sent down to Hardwick in September 1635, and also such miscellaneous items as coal baskets, brooms and rushes, as well as the tapes, webbing, stuffing and stiffening needed for upholstery, together with the necessary fittings, including tenter hooks, curtain rings and rods. In late September 1635 '2 peeces of Ticking to make Chayres and Stools at Hardwicke' were bought for £1 12s from an unknown source, but probably from Collins, since, in November, he was paid 10s 6d for 'sacking, tape and other thinges mentioned in his byll for making up of the Chayres and stooles in the upper great Chamber at Hardwicke'.

Although Collins made up the set, he was not responsible for its covers, which were of velvet with applied flowers and other motifs of needlework. These were supplied by the embroiderer George Savage, who was paid £1 15s 'for seaven weekes worke done about the chaires and stools in the upper great chamber at Hardwicke'. This is a low figure, especially compared with the £123 6s 10d paid to an embroiderer called Booth for eight weeks' work from 14 July to 7 September 1635. Booth must have been a high-class metal-thread embroiderer, and his bill would have included the cost of the materials. Savage was probably simply applying the ready-made motifs, which can still be seen in the High Great Chamber on the replacement chairs and stools (see **75**).

Two items were noted as being specifically for Christian Bruce's use at Hardwick. One was a 'black sheet for my La:' Bed', towards which two separate payments of 8s and £3 were recorded. The sheet, which was presumably for the black bed mentioned above, would have been of fine linen decorated with black embroidery, worked, in this instance, not with silk but with fine crewel (worsted) wool, which had cost £1 16s. The other item was a 'couche bedde for the lower drawinge roome at Hardwicke', for which Stephen Collins supplied 7 yards of cloth to cover the padding for the modest sum of 5s 3d; there is no identifiable entry for the main upholstery fabric.[10] While Stephen Collins was working on the couch bed at Hardwick, he was paid for various other things, including bed cords, pack thread, curtain rods for the 'upper drawing chamber window', and 8s 6d for his travel. This was common practice and, in September 1635, for example, he was paid 4s 4d for 'calling to help make a curtaine for the blew bed at Leicester' – perhaps the one now at Hardwick.

Christian Bruce purchased silks of the same type as those bought by Bess: satin, velvet, taffeta, sarcenet and damask. In addition to the blue damask bed, she also had one of crimson damask for which a new bedstead was bought for a modest £2 7s 6d in January 1636/7. By comparison, an unknown quantity of red figured satin purchased for use on a bed and matching furniture cost £36 1s 6d. Satin was usually a plain fabric, but by the early seventeenth century it was also available with small patterns brocaded in gold and silver. The hangings in Arbella's room in 1601 – of 'satten wroughte with golde flowers and trees' – may have been early examples.

As in the sixteenth century, considerable quantities of wool were used – scarlet kersey (or carsey), yellow bays and purple saye, of which Collins supplied 17 yards at 2s 4d a yard in November 1635. By the seventeenth century, saye was sometimes woven with a silk warp sized to give it a sheen. Yet another wool was rashe; a twill-woven fabric of mixed carded and combed wool, made with or without a nap in varying qualities. In June 1637, 21 yards of green rashe were bought 'For my lady's closet', perhaps to make loose covers for the furniture, since 39⅛ yards of green silk fringe were bought at the same time; the fringe cost £7 3s 2d and the rashe only £2 12s 6d. A new pure cotton or mixed cotton and linen fabric used by Christian Bruce was vermilion, of which 90 yards were bought in March 1637 to make a bed. According to Lewis Roberts, writing in 1641, it was made in Manchester from imported cotton wool bought in London.[11] The quantity needed shows why a silk bed, fully lined and complete with silk or metal *passementerie*, was so expensive.

Christian Bruce clearly enjoyed needlework, just as Bess had done, and much of the applied canvas work at Hardwick, like that on the chairs and stools in the High Great Chamber, dates from her time (see **75**). Sadly, however, none of the finer embroidery commissioned by her has survived.[12] It included the tawny velvet bed embroidered with gold and silver thread, a satin bed worked with coloured silks, a set of purple kersey hangings embroidered in white silk and the vermilion bed, which was worked with fine crewel wool that cost £4 8s 9d compared to the £7 9s 9d spent on the 90 yards of fabric.

An interesting reference in Christian Bruce's accounts is to carpets made of heavy woven fabrics, including double cloths, something that was to become common in the later eighteenth century (see pp.92–3). She bought two double shaft carpets and four single shaft carpets in March 1637, together with some 'Bristow stuffe', which would have been heavy worsted fabric from the West Country sold via Bristol. Her father-in-law, the 1st Earl, had Bristow carpeting in his London house in 1617, but he was using it at the windows,[13] and Christian Bruce may have followed suit rather than put her woven carpets on the floor. During the three-year period covered by the account book, she also bought one unspecified type of 'great Carpett' for £11 17s 8d, which was perhaps second-hand or flat-woven, since she paid £14 for an English turkey-work carpet. It is not clear whether they were intended for the floor or a table.

In the seventeenth century, as in the sixteenth, the provision of an adequate supply of household linen was a major preoccupation. In the period March 1635 to September 1637, 22 yards of linen was bought specifically for Hardwick, provided by Stephen Collins, and another 22 yards of coarser cloth were purchased for sheets from his wife. Rather more expensive linen included a pair of flaxen sheets at 16s the pair, a dozen diaper napkins at 9s 6d, and two diaper cloths at 11s 4d. In addition, other large quantities were purchased, presumably for distribution to the various houses as need arose. These included 233 yards of flaxen cloth of varying lengths and qualities, costing in total £22 4s 2d. Chatsworth and Leicester Abbey seem to have received more linen than Hardwick during this particular period, but the best linen was undoubtedly bought for the London house, in particular for the visit of King Charles in May 1636.[14]

There were also bills for making up the linen: 26 dozen diaper napkins were made and marked for 16s, and 10 dozen hall napkins were made for 7s 6d. Ready-made napkins cost 6–7s the dozen. Another item of household expenditure detailed in the accounts was the cost of laundry; the washing of 38 pairs of sheets and 2 pairs of pillow cases, for example, cost 13s. The need to heat large quantities of water made washing a major undertaking and in most great houses at this time it was not a weekly chore, but one spread over several days at intervals of a month or more, hence the payment to 'a woman that helped to wash 6 days, 4s 4d'.

By 1638, when her son William came of age, Christian Bruce's careful management enabled her to hand over to him 'his great houses in Derbyshire, all ready furnished. She herself living in that of Leicester Abbey'.[15] This satisfactory state of affairs was not to last, however; in 1641 the first Civil War broke out and, in 1642, William Cavendish joined the King at York. His estates were sequestered and he temporarily went into exile, but he returned in 1645 and made his peace with Parliament. From then until the Restoration in 1660, he lived quietly, moving, as his privy purse accounts show, between London, his uncle's house at Ampthill, Bedfordshire, and his mother's house at Roehampton just west of London.[16] He also visited Hardwick and Chatsworth, which had been briefly occupied by both sides during the wars. Although not fully in control of his estates, the 3rd Earl was not short of money. His personal expenses were between £800 and £1,000 a year, spent mostly on clothes, travel, books and miscellaneous gifts, such as the £10 he gave to his old tutor Thomas Hobbes in March 1654/5.

In 1660, with the restoration of Charles II, all the restrictions imposed by Parliament were removed and the Earl took up residence at Chatsworth. There is little information about his expenditure on his houses, but the black japanned day-bed and chairs with squabs of pink silk embroidered in silver date from his time, although it is not known for which house they were first acquired.[17] Furnishings continued to be moved between the houses, just as they had been in the sixteenth century. In 1675, after the death of Christian Bruce, her house at Roehampton was given up, and an inventory was taken of the tapestries there, at Southampton House in London and 'also what hangings was formerly at Devonshire Ho. without Bishopsgate'.[18] There was a total of 165 pieces, not all of which are described, but there were at least 42 pieces of 'Forrest Work', and 14 of 'Beastes'. Of the named sets, most had been split, not simply between rooms in each house, but between the houses: the *Hercules* and *Alexander* sets were split between Southampton and Devonshire Houses, and the fourteen-piece set of *David and Uriah* was distributed between all three houses. There was obviously a great move around of the sets at this time, including the five-piece set of *Hero and Leander*, which was to surface again at Hardwick two hundred years later (**78**). It now hangs on the lower section of the Great Staircase, having been brought from Chatsworth by the 6th Duke.

78 *Hero mourning over the dead Leander* from a set of five tapestry hangings woven at Mortlake in the mid-17th century. They are recorded in an inventory of the Cavendish London Houses taken in 1675 and were eventually moved to Hardwick by the 6th Duke. They now hang on the lower section of the main staircase. (350 × 420cm) Inv. T.142b *NTPL*

79 Detail of a game of croquet from a set of four tapestries of *Playing Boys*, also known as *The Polidors*. They were based on paintings by Polidoro da Caravaggio (1490–1535) which had been purchased by Charles I, patron of the Mortlake tapestry works. One panel is marked FP HATTON GARDEN for Francis Poyntz, Yeoman Arrasmaker to Charles II, who also ran a workshop in Hatton Garden, London, *c.*1670–1684. They may have been bought new or acquired second hand at a later date. (approx 230 × 220cm) T/96d *NTPL/John Hammond*

The 3rd Earl seems to have preferred living at Chatsworth with his books and scholarly pursuits, but he also began to find the Tudor building old-fashioned and inconvenient. Between 1678 and 1680 he installed a new staircase and replaced the old mullions with sash windows. This tinkering with the house was to be taken a great deal further by his son William, who succeeded him as 4th Earl in 1684. He was, like his father, a Fellow of the Royal Society and he had a talent for music and a taste for painting and architecture. According to Bishop Burnet, he was 'of a nice honour in everything but the paying of his tradesmen'.[19]

The 4th Earl also played an important role in the constitutional changes of the late seventeenth century which resulted in the English crown being offered to William of Orange and his wife Mary, daughter of James II. This service brought him financial rewards and honours culminating in his creation as Marquess of Hartington and 1st Duke of Devonshire in 1694. He had by then already begun making improvements to Chatsworth, starting in 1687 with the simple idea of putting a modern front on the south side of the house, but one thing led to another and, for almost as long as Bess had taken to build the house, he worked at its transformation; the final, north front was finished shortly before his death in 1707. In addition, he built a new Devonshire House in Piccadilly and the two together must have resulted in a monumental move around of furniture and furnishings, from which none of his houses can have escaped, least of all Hardwick, which provided a convenient base from which to oversee his work when Chatsworth was uninhabitable.[20]

It was probably the 1st Duke, rather than his father, who altered the rooms on the first floor at Hardwick to create two quite separate suites for himself and his wife. It was at this time that Tobies Room (now the Cut-Velvet Dressing Room) was converted into a closet (81) with moulded frames surrounding fitted fabric panels (but not the present ones) and

80 (*left*) Georgiana, Duchess of Devonshire, with her eldest daughter, painted by Reynolds in 1784–5. Georgiana (1757–1806) was the daughter of the 1st Earl Spencer and wife of the 5th Duke of Devonshire. *Devonshire Collection*

81 (*right*) Dressing Room to the Cut-Velvet Room showing the panelled walls, Baroque mouldings and fire surround which were introduced when the room was converted into a private closet in the late 17th century. The needlework wall panels, carpet and hearth rug were introduced in the mid- to late 19th century (see figs. **88** and **96**). *NTPL*

elaborate carving round the doors and fireplace; it must have made a cosy and comfortable private room, despite its northern aspect.

As work on Chatsworth continued, the State Rooms, including those of the Earl of Leicester and the Queen of Scots, were swept away, although the old names were retained. It is unlikely that the canopy of velvet and cloth of gold – the only important furnishing left in those rooms in 1601 – had survived until the end of the century, but Hardwick was the likely resting place for the many furnishings made redundant as the new house emerged. Among the furnishings purchased in their place was a state bed hung with red velvet embroidered with raised metal-thread work which, by 1764, was in the Queen of Scots Bedchamber. The name stuck, and when the bed was later moved to Hardwick (see **95**), it was called her bed, despite the presence of ducal coronets on its feet – as the 6th Duke delighted in pointing out. A second grand bed was bought in 1697 from the upholsterer Francis Lapierre,[21] for the large sum of £470, which was paid off at £6 a week, and this bed too was eventually dismantled and the headcloth and tester now form the canopy of state in the Gallery at Hardwick (see **90**). With such wholesale rebuilding, it was not only the textiles that were moved; sections of panelling, probably including the inlaid work in the chapel altar rail, the intarsia panels now on the Chapel Stairs and the panel with the arms of Mary Queen of Scots, were taken to Hardwick, where they helped to support the association between her and the house that became accepted as fact in the eighteenth century.[22]

The New Hall at Hardwick had been built and furnished according to the ideas of suitability and lasting worth that Bess had absorbed in the mid-sixteenth century, and the attitudes to ceremony represented by her State Rooms were to remain valid well into the seventeenth century and were respected for much longer. The less formal rooms, however, soon began to reflect changing styles and codes of conduct which were summed up by the 1st Duke's remodelling of Chatsworth. By the time of his death in 1707 the contrast between Chatsworth and Hardwick was striking and the differences were to be strengthened by developments in the eighteenth century. Chatsworth had become the family's preferred country house, but it was not their main place of residence. The introduction of annual parliaments helped create the London Season, which lasted, by the end of the eighteenth century, from October to April. In addition, there were the attractions of various spas, both in Britain and on the Continent, while the family's houses increased in number with the marriage in 1748 of the future 4th Duke to Lady Charlotte Boyle, heiress to the 3rd Earl of Burlington. She brought with her estates in Ireland and Yorkshire, as well as Burlington House in London and Chiswick House near the Thames. By the time of the 5th Duke (succeeded 1764-1811), it was calculated that whereas his grandfather had spent nine months of the year at Chatsworth and his father six months, he was there for no more than three.[23]

If Chatsworth was often silent, how much quieter must Hardwick have been; yet this infrequent use, coupled with a disinclination for radical change on the part of the 2nd and 3rd Dukes (1707-29, 1729-55), saved the house from either drastic improvement or destruction. By the time of the 4th Duke (1755-64), who was more actively involved with his houses, other influences were working in Hardwick's favour; they included a growing interest in antiquarianism, landscape and the Gothic style.

When the 4th Duke turned his attention to Hardwick, the most noticeable thing he did was to demolish part of the Old Hall, although he was not, as Horace Walpole stated in his *Journal*, intent on 'pulling the whole down'.[24] Not only was the extra space still needed to accommodate the staff who accompanied the family on their visits, but the irregular silhouette created by his work may have been an intentional response to contemporary

enthusiasms. Perched on the edge of an escarpment, the Old Hall provided a picturesque image much admired by the increasing number of travellers who came to enjoy the Derbyshire scenery and to visit its houses.[25] Horace Walpole visited both houses in September 1760, but he refused to be 'charmed' by Hardwick, 'as I had been promised'. He condemned the New Hall for 'not being Gothic', and would not have endeared himself to its creator by describing her great rooms as 'vast chambers such as nobility of that time delighted in, and did not know how to furnish'. Walpole was excited, however, by his mistaken belief that 'the great apartment is exactly what it was when the Queen of Scots was kept there'.[26] This myth, which the family seems to have nurtured, heightened the interest and enjoyment of the visitors and it may have helped the preservation of the older embroideries, particularly those in the State Rooms, that came to be identified with the Scottish Queen. But, despite this, the furnishings continued to be altered and rearranged as is shown by three inventories taken in 1764, 1792 and 1811.[27]

The first inventory, made on the death of the 4th Duke, is fairly brief, but it shows by the increase in the number of attic rooms and the move of the first set of appliqué hangings to the present Cut-Velvet Rooms, that it was the 4th Duke who had lowered the ceiling of the Withdrawing Chamber (**82**).[28] Elsewhere, however, despite the brevity of the descriptions, contemporary comment confirms that some of the original furnishings remained *in situ*. One of the most important rooms, the State Chamber (the Best Bedchamber of 1601 and, today, the Green Velvet Room), contained 'A very old Bed with hangings' and, on the walls, 'Old Hangings, velvet & work'd', which are confirmed as those listed in the 1601 inventory by Walpole's description of 1760: the 'Hangings are embroidered on black & white velvet with allegoric & historic figures large as life'.[29] Later inventories and comments confirm that, in addition to the hangings and the bed, at least three other of the room's original textile furnishings were still there, although in 1764 they were either inadequately described or were temporarily in the chest in the Wardrobe 'wth. sundry pieces of Fine wor'd Things in it'.

Several sets of tapestry are likely to have remained in their original locations, but they

82 The Withdrawing Room in an 1820s watercolour by William Hunt. The ceiling of this former State Room (see pp.33-5) was originally as high as those of the Gallery and High Great Chamber but was lowered by the 4th Duke in the 1750s. Later in the 18th century it became a bedroom and in the 19th century the 6th Duke converted it into a Library. To the left of the fireplace is one of the 16th-century long cushions mounted in a screen. *Devonshire Collection*

83 The Blue Bedroom showing the replica bed mounted with some of the needlework motifs from the blue damask bed that belonged to Christian Bruce, wife of the 2nd Earl. Her arms and the date 1629 are applied to the headcloth together with those of the 6th Duke and the date 1852. The pattern of the damask is based, not on that of the original bed (fig. **77**), but on a silk of the mid- 18th century. *NTPL/Nadia MacKenzie*

were not named and Walpole's comment on seeing at Chatsworth 'six pieces of Tapestry brought from Hardwick, after Designs of Rubens or Snyder', is a salutory reminder that furnishings continued to be moved about and that many new furnishings had been introduced at Hardwick during the seventeenth and early eighteenth centuries.[30]

Christian Bruce's stewardship is represented in the 1764 inventory by her two canopies of state, her couch, her set of stools and chairs in the High Great Chamber and possibly by the bed with 'Blew damask Hangings, a Counterpoint for it', in what, for the first recorded time, was called the Blue Bed Chamber (originally the Pearl Bedchamber). There is some doubt because the bed was no longer there in 1792, while in 1811 there were two blue damask beds at Hardwick.[31] Either the two beds were subsequently confused, or Christian Bruce's bed had already undergone substantial alteration, because when the 6th Duke had the bed remade in 1852, he copied a mid-eighteenth century damask, not the curving sprig motif seen on an unaltered valance from the original bed of 1629 (see **77**). The seventeenth-century applied needlework was reused. According to Bishop White Kennett the bed in the Queen of Scots Room had been 'taken away for Plunder during the Civil Wars', and, by 1764, it had been replaced by a 'white work'd bed', which has been assumed to be the bed drawn by S. H. Grimm in 1785[32] and which, as already discussed, incorporates part of the 1601 Best Bed (see p.73). By 1792, the white worked bed had gone and the Queen of Scots Room contained a bed 'with Needlework Hangings'. Without a better description, identification cannot be certain, but it might be the bed with 'Curtains pan'd wt. Velvet & needleworks, a Needle work Counterpain wt. Gold Silver & Silk', which was in the Needlework Bed Chamber at Chatsworth in 1764, but not in 1792. By

1811, the needlework bed had vanished, but curtains matching the description now hang at either side of the Hall Gallery, with four more in store. They date from about 1700.

In 1811, the Queen of Scots Room (**84**) had a black velvet bed with applied needlework motifs. This had been moved from the present Cut-Velvet Room where it was recorded in 1764, to the Blue Bedroom by 1792, and, had it not been the bed stolen in the Civil War, it might even have incorporated some of the motifs from the original needlework bed recorded there in 1601. The present bed is a nineteenth-century re-creation of the eighteenth-century bed, using sixteenth- and seventeenth-century motifs.

Not only do the three inventories provide useful information about the sixteenth-century pieces, but they help chart the changing fashions in textile furnishings that affected first Chatsworth, and then Hardwick. By 1764, the late seventeenth-century state bed, hung with crimson velvet embroidered with gold and silver, at Chatsworth had been moved within the house to the Queen of Scots Apartment and replaced with a more restrained bed of crimson damask bound with gold braid, parts of which are now in store at Hardwick. The 4th Duke's own mahogany bed at Chatsworth was hung with printed cotton lined with white, and, throughout the house, there were beds of chintz, printed cotton, blue and white and red and white check, with 'washing quilts', in place of the elaborate counterpoints of earlier periods.[33]

Older 'stuff beds' of wool were in the maids' rooms in the attics, which were hung with tapestry, and although 'Hang's of very fine tapestry' remained in the Drawing Room and most of the State Rooms, elsewhere the walls were covered with striped satin, red silk, and paper edged with gold. Among the upholstered furniture were settees as well as arm

84 The Queen of Scots Room in an 1820s watercolour by William Hunt. The black velvet bed is similar to that now in the room, although the needlework motifs on the upper valance have been remounted in a slightly different order and the lower valances are quite different. The valances and coverlet were probably 19th century window drapes. The needlework borders match those on Christian Bruce's bed (figs. **77** and **83**) and the size of the slips suggest that they too had been worked in the 17th century. *Devonshire Collection*

85 Bed in the Lawn Room; linen embroidered with crewel (worsted) wool in stem, buttonhole, double-back, brick, chain, detached chain and speckling stitches. The hangings, which date from the early 18th century, were altered in the late 19th century, when some additional pieces were worked, for example the tabs on the upper valances. A left-over and still unfaded panel is in store. Inv. F/471 *NTPL/Nadia MacKenzie*

chairs, almost all covered with silk damask, although some had embroidered covers worked in tent and cross stitch (see **98**). These were about to go out of fashion, and one set of 'twelve nedle worked chairs wt. green covers' was already in store. Protective loose covers of printed cotton or striped linen and a few of silk damask were now provided for all upholstered items; they were removed only on formal occasions.

At Hardwick, the attics were also hung with 'old Tapestry', and the only bed there, like many lower down the house, had 'old blue cutains', 'green stuff curtains' and curtains of 'striped stuff'. The hangings of the bed in the 'Work'd Bed Chamber' – assuming it was the crewel-work bed still in the house – dated from the early eighteenth century (**85**). The description of the 4th Duke's private rooms is tantalisingly close to that of Bess's and Arbella's Chambers in 1601. His bed was hung with 'Red cloth', and tapestries clothed the walls, while the Dressing Room had hangings of damask, as Arbella's room had done. Although the original furnishings must have been replaced in the late seventeenth century, if not earlier, the use of red bed hangings – of wool or silk – seems to have become a tradition, and Bess's Bedchamber was sometimes called 'The Scarlet Cloth Room'.

In general, the furniture recorded in 1764 was old – oak tables with textile covers, japanned chests, chairs with caned seats and backs, and others with covers of carpeting, perhaps made from seventeenth-century turkey-work (**86**). Only in the Drawing Room were there hints of greater refinement in the tea table and 'tea things', a settee and twelve chairs upholstered in green damask with striped linen covers. These perhaps dated from the time of the 3rd Duke's wife, for the 4th Duke was a widower and in 1764 there was no separate set of rooms for a Duchess.

The 4th Duke's early death stopped any further work he may have planned for the

86 Accumulated furniture: two stools (a plain 17th century one and another made from a cut-down chair *c.*1700) both upholstered with English turkey-work cut from carpets *c.*1600; a late 17th century walnut arm chair with pieced but contemporary turkey-work upholstery; a stool from a set matching the red velvet state bed moved from the Queen of Scots' Apartment at Chatsworth *c.*1700 – the worn silver-thread embroidery has been re-mounted on a later cushion; an 18th-century dining chair with a case cover of 19th-century printed cotton. Inv. F/441, F/335, F/342, F/340, F/536 *NTPL/Nadia MacKenzie*

house. His son, the 5th Duke, was only sixteen when he succeeded to the title, and it was not until after his marriage in 1774 to Georgiana Spencer, daughter of the 1st Earl Spencer of Althorp, that more attention was paid to his houses. His principal residence was Devonshire House in Piccadilly, where the young Duchess, a legendary leader of fashion, enchanted society (**80**). She and the Duke spent part of their honeymoon at Chatsworth and she remained deeply attached to it and Hardwick, as did her mother Lady Spencer, and her sister Harriet, Lady Bessborough. Throughout her short, strangely complicated and restless life, Georgiana continued to return with relief to Derbyshire, and on 15 November 1786, for example, she wrote to her mother from Hardwick, where she had been since October: 'We remain here about 3 weeks longer, Bess and us, we then go for a week to Chatsworth, and then for about 3 weeks to Buxton, then D[st], we are to move southwards'.[34] However intermittently Hardwick was visited by Georgiana and other members of her family, including her three children, the house had always to be kept in readiness for them.

The 5th Duke spent lavishly on his houses; Chatsworth underwent major refurbishment in 1786 and work on Hardwick followed in the late 1780s. Both are recorded in a journal kept by the Hon. John Byng (later 5th Viscount Torrington) during a tour made in June 1789.[35] He was completely bowled over by Hardwick:

On a lofty hill crown'd with wood, and looking like a great, old castle of romance, stood seated, Hardwick Hall – the 1st object of our ride. . . . I was highly pleased to find myself mistaken in having supposed it a deserted ruin; as much repair has been done within some last years, and many masons here now at work inside.

87 Drawing made in 1785 by S. H. Grimm of the plain canopy installed in the Gallery since the inventory taken in 1764. It shows a plain canopy trimmed only with a fringe and two applied panels of embroidery. Below it are Christian Bruce's couch equipped with new seat furniture, and two stools, possibly also re-upholstered 17th-century pieces.

He and his companions were shown round by the Housekeeper and he found much to admire on the second floor: 'a profusion of fine apartments with painted oak doors and lofty mantlepieces; all hung with tapestry, except those of Mary; whose work of gold figures upon black silks and velvets, for hangings, still cover the walls.' He was rather critical of the new woodwork and was of the opinion 'that the first expense about this house, were I to command, wou'd be an allotment of some £3,000 for carpets and grates', but he left feeling that 'I never did and probably never shall see such another house of antiquity'. By comparison, at Chatsworth he condemned 'all the foolish glare, uncomfortable rooms, and frippery French furniture at this vile house'. Chatsworth continued to be modernised, as the inventories of 1792 and 1811 record, but the situation at Hardwick was different and, as John Byng perceptively summed it up: 'Hardwick House, a house of grandeur, as a house of comfort is worth a dozen Chatsworths', for although it was generally better furnished and more comfortable by 1792 than it had been for some years, it was not fashionable.

The most substantial changes recorded at Hardwick in 1792 were in the service areas. A housekeeper's room appeared for the first time, comfortably furnished with an easy chair covered with carpeting. There were three staff bedrooms on the ground floor equipped with furniture moved from Chatsworth, as were the smaller rooms on the first floor and the eight attics allocated to the footmen. The house was thus better prepared for the necessary staff who accompanied visiting members of the family, who still lived mainly on the first floor.[36]

These rooms showed fewer changes: the Drawing Room still contained the twelve chairs upholstered in green damask with blue and white linen covers, but now described as 'old', and the old arm chair and settee of 1764 might have been concealed beneath the green and white covers of the easy chair and sofa recorded in 1792. However, the 'confidente' with a cover of red and white stripes was new to the house, as was the pianoforte and a large Wilton carpet. The Dining Room had acquired a large Turkish carpet, a larger table and a set of eighteen mahogany chairs with plain seats. By 1811 the chairs, which are still in the room, were described as having seats upholstered 'in Sattin Hair Cloth', that is, a tough satin-weave fabric incorporating horse-hair, probably woven in Norwich (**29**). The bed in 'Their Graces' Bedroom' (Bess's bedchamber) still had red cloth hangings, but these were probably newly imported, since they were 'ornamented with silver' and lined with 'yellow Persian', a lightweight plain silk. There were two Wilton bedside carpets.

The crewelwork bed of 1764 (see **85**) was still in place but, as already noted, the black velvet bed, in what is now the Cut-Velvet Room, had been moved upstairs (see p.87). It was replaced by a 'French bedstead with Mahogany poles and yellow and white striped cotton furniture', formerly at Chatsworth. The room also had a large Scotch carpet, two bedside carpets and a floor mat – John Byng would have approved. The Withdrawing Chamber was now fitted out as a bedroom with a chintz bed from the Leicester Rooms at Chatsworth and a second small mahogany bureau bed which had yellow and white check curtains and a white cotton quilt.[37] There were eleven chairs covered in carpeting, a new floor mat and two bedside carpets. The room must have made a disturbing contrast with the adjacent High Great Chamber, which remained largely unaltered except for the loss of a table with a cover and the addition of more furniture, including chairs from one of the blue damask suites, as well as the seventeenth-century japanned day-bed and matching chairs with caned seats and loose cushions of pink satin. The Gallery was relatively unchanged, although Christian Bruce's canopy of state (described as 'old' in 1764) had been replaced by a very plain one shown by Grimm in a drawing of 1785 (**87**).

Although new decorative schemes were never imposed on Hardwick, the inventories record the influence of changing styles, as outdated furniture was moved across from Chatsworth, and within the house there was a steady progression from the first and second floors down to the ground floor and then up to the attics of woollen furnishings, then of silk and then of chintz and printed cottons. Some of the grander items, notably the beds, remained *in situ* for longer but, in general, a tide of printed cotton and checked linen and cotton had spread throughout the house by 1811. Even the attics had been stripped of their tapestry hangings, but the turrets on the roof now contained 'A quantity of old ragged tapestry'.

Window and Floor Coverings

Throughout the life of the house, a major indicator of changing ideas of style and comfort lay in the treatment of the floors and windows. In the sixteenth century, window curtains were relatively rare and although the New Hall had been equipped with some, they were mostly thin ones to filter the strong light, or substantial blankets to keep out some of the cold, although the Gallery, the Withdrawing Chamber, the Best Bedchamber and the High Great Chamber had no curtains at all. None the less, on 4 March 1603 Bess's granddaughter Arbella described going up to the High Great Chamber and finding a group of attendants 'takeing the advantage of the fire to warme by till the sunne shining on our world with hotter and farther distant beames make it need-lesse'.[38] Few people who now experience the room in early March would consider a fire and curtains needless.

By 1764 there were 'old window curtains' in most of the second-floor rooms and, by 1792, when window drapery was on the way to becoming a complex art form, things had progressed to the degree that simple 'sliding window curtains' were found only in the less important rooms. The family's rooms now had 'draw-up curtains' mostly of green 'china', and some of crimson damask. China was an alternative name for cheney, a worsted furnishing fabric, sometimes watered. None the less, the Duchess Georgiana described how 'The wind is wonderfully high, and according to the custom of all old houses, our window curtains are about four yards too short, & of the consistency of table cloths, which is rather thin, as there are no shutters anywhere in the house', but, she added, 'we are to have some reasonable curtains by Monday next' – she also continued to stay in the house in winter.[39] By 1811, however, the Dining Room had been fitted with 'a very large Green Haraton festoon window curtain, 2 lessor size festoon window curtains, 2 Green baize curtains with laths and Rods', and there were festoon curtains in several other rooms, including crimson silk ones in the Drawing Room. The 6th Duke, who succeeded to the title that year, was to increase the comfort levels still further.

In 1601 the majority of the floors at Hardwick had been covered by rush matting, which provided a relatively soft and warm surface, although, as now, it wore out. Arbella Stuart wrote, in the letter quoted above, of walking with her cousin Mary Talbot 'in the great chamber, for feare of wearing the mattes in the Gallery (reserved for you Courtyers)'.[40] Later inventories show that matting was still the norm and the 6th Duke recorded that, even at Chatsworth, the Drawing Room 'was matted like Hardwick', when he inherited the title.[41] Unlike Hardwick, Chatsworth had many fine wooden floors suitable for the display of a large central carpet, a fashion increasingly common from the mid-eighteenth century onwards.[42] By that time, hand-knotted European carpets were available, including English ones from Fulham, Moorfields, Exeter and Axminster in

88 Floor coverings: rush matting of a type used since the house was built; a flat broad-loom double-cloth carpet woven in the late 19th century but technically similar to those recorded in Bess's Bedchamber in 1601 and in the accounts of the 1st Earl and Christian Bruce; on top of it are three examples of 19th-century strip carpeting: a piece of cut-pile Wilton carpet with an added needlework border; a hearth mat (see fig. **83**) and two (joined) unfaded off-cuts from a border – all of Brussels loop-pile carpeting. Inv. T/20, T/340, T/362, T/461
NTPL/John Hammond

Devon and although oriental carpets were still imported, interest in them declined from the 1770s onwards, as interiors began to be designed as a whole, including the major furnishings. The 6th Duke was to write approvingly of the English carpets at Chatsworth, which were 'made at Axminster, and they wear much better and fade less than the French'.[43] By the time carpets were introduced to Hardwick in any quantity, however, the hand-knotted variety was losing ground to carpets woven on the same principle as velvet, with the raised loops either left uncut or cut to form a pile. The former type was called Brussels, where the technique is said to have originated, and the cut-pile version was known as Wilton, where it had first been made in the 1740s. It was subsequently made at Kidderminster, in Worcestershire, and elsewhere (**88**).

Flat-woven carpeting had first been used in the house in 1601, when Bess had a crewel-wool floorspread by her bed, but, although the 1st Earl and Christian Bruce bought quite a lot in the early seventeenth century, it seems not to have been used on the floor, and it was not until the later eighteenth century that it came into widespread use. It was made in several centres in England and Scotland, but the names Kidderminster and Scotch were

89 View of the High Great Chamber from P. Robinson's *New Vitruvius Britannicus* of 1835. The floor is fitted with strip carpeting, Christian Bruce's canopy is on the far wall and, in the window recess, is the state bed brought from the Queen of Scots apartment at Chatsworth. *NT*

used generically; the 1811 inventory describes a 'Kidderminster Scotch Bedside Carpet' in one of the rooms. All these carpets were woven in narrow strips, usually 27 inches wide, but sometimes as much as 36 inches. The strips could be seamed together to make large central carpets finished with specially woven borders, which were also used when strip carpeting was fitted to the room, as in the Dressing Room to the Scarlet Cloth Bedroom (the name for Bess's old bedchamber); in 1811 this had 'a Kidderminster carpet planned to the floor'.

Fitted strip carpeting soon replaced rush matting in most of the rooms and it can be seen in an engraving of the High Great Chamber published in P. Robinson's *New Vitruvius Britannicus* of 1835 (**89**), while an 1840s watercolour by David Cox shows joined strips covering a large portion of the Gallery. Hardwick was also equipped with another form of strip carpeting, called Venetian; this was usually patterned with stripes in a warp-faced weave. In the nineteenth century it was used almost exclusively for stairs and corridors, but the several Venetian carpets and 'bedsides', mentioned in the 1811 inventory suggest that it had had a wider use in the eighteenth century.

Despite the slow modernisation of Hardwick, a nucleus of old furniture and textile furnishings still survived from the sixteenth and seventeenth centuries and in some instances can be clearly identified in the later inventories. In 1811, for example, there was in the Drawing Room 'A japanned pole fire-screen with an Embroidered pink Sattin and Gold Veil lin'd with Grey silk fringed and tassels'. This had been made by roughly sewing together the ends of the two cushion covers, lined with blue Chinese damask, which had originally been in the Gallery (see **59**). Because of this bizarre use, they remained otherwise unaltered until they were separated for display in the late 1980s.

Chapter Five

THE 6TH DUKE
AND BEYOND

T he 6th Duke, who inherited the vast Devonshire estates at the age of 21 in 1811, had a propensity for extravagance passed down from both his parents, and within a very short time his balls and dinners at Devonshire House were as famous as his house parties at Chatsworth were to be later. In 1820, he began the improvement and enlargement of Chatsworth that was to continue for twenty years and which was also to affect Hardwick.

The 6th Duke had a great affection for both houses but he seems to have loved Hardwick as the more private house, of which he had happy childhood memories. His two sisters were equally fond of it, and in November 1820 Harriet, Lady Granville, wrote to Georgiana, Lady Morpeth: 'We found Hart [6th Duke] who will write to you about Hardwick for the beginning of December. If it can be achieved what happiness it will be!' It was achieved and she no doubt spoke for them all when she wrote from Hardwick on 14 December: 'I have been so happy here that I feel an unreasonable sorrow at going the day after tomorrow.'[1]

Perhaps this deep affection enabled the Duke to respond to the atmosphere and needs of the house in a way he failed to do at Chatsworth. He wrote with concern of tapestry 'all in rags, so very much decayed, that I feel obliged with great regret, to remove it', although this did not stop him cutting out the best bits and using them like wallpaper around the house.[2] But at least he started from the premise that Hardwick should be preserved and that the dreadful process of decay should be halted. He lived long before textile conservation had become a skilled profession and his methods were those of a Victorian housekeeper and skilled upholsterer. Here he had the help of John Gregory Crace who, from 1840 onwards, worked on transforming the interiors of several of the Duke's houses, and it was into his hands that the Duke put the two sets of *The Virtues*, when he removed them from the present Cut-Velvet and Green Velvet Rooms, where one set had hung since the late 1590s. After their repair, the six remaining panels were hung in the High Great Chamber on easel-like frames, which provided inadequate support and no protection, yet they stayed there until the 1890s when Lady Egerton, daughter of the 7th Duke, installed them in unglazed screens in the Hall (see **97**).

The rooms from which *The Virtues* had come were refurbished, and their beds of crimson damask replaced, in one case by the present cut-velvet bed (**91**), which had been made by Thomas Vardy for the 3rd Duke in about 1740, and which was moved across from the Leicester Apartment at Chatsworth.[3] The walls of both rooms were hung with Flemish tapestries brought from Chatsworth, although those in the Cut-Velvet Room did not then include the present two panels depicting the *Prodigal Son*. These were hung in the Duke's Dressing Room, and he noted that 'there are people here who can remember that the Prodigal Son was in one of the turrets'. His room also contained the *Judgement of Paris* table carpet and, opposite the fireplace, 'a piece of needlework that, I am assured by good authority, neither love nor money could now procure. I think it must have been Indian

90 Section of the Gallery in a watercolour painted by David Cox *c*.1840. It shows the canopy from the red damask state bed supplied for Chatsworth by Francis Lapierre in 1697. Below it is Christian Bruce's couch, re-upholstered in silk damask (the remains of which are visible in a photograph of *c*.1900). The red curtains at the windows were introduced by the 6th Duke and the floor is covered with matting and carpets. *Devonshire Collection*

91 (*left*) View of the Cut-Velvet Room. The bed, made by Thomas Vardy for the 3rd Earl in 1740, is of cut and uncut silk velvet on a white ribbed silk ground. Inv. F/424
NTPL/Nadia MacKenzie

92 (*right*) The green velvet bed in what was originally the Best Bedchamber; cut and uncut silk velvet on a green satin ground. The early 18th-century bed was brought from Londesborough in Yorkshire – a house that had come into the family with the marriage of the future 4th Duke to Lady Charlotte Boyle, heiress to the 3rd Earl of Burlington. Inv. F/321 *NTPL/John Hammond*

patience alone that could execute such a thing.'[4] This was presumably one of the two Indian coverlets that remain in the house (see p.28).

In the former Best Bedchamber, the Duke hung the *Abraham* set, apparently unaware that it had originally been the second set for the Withdrawing Chamber. He also installed there an early eighteenth-century green velvet bed (**92**) from Londesborough, Yorkshire, a house which had come to the Devonshires as a result of the 4th Duke's marriage and which the 6th Duke had sold in 1840. Many of its contents were taken to Chatsworth, where they joined the large accumulation of furnishings on which he drew in dressing-up Hardwick. Among this material was an enchanting late eighteenth-century Neo-classical bed with white hangings embroidered with deep pink silk in coral stitch, a knotted stitch that echoes the delicate fringes of knotted thread with which they are trimmed (**94**). The bed had probably belonged to the Duke's mother Georgiana and it is tempting to think that she may even have worked some of the knotting. Horace Walpole, in commenting on her love of gambling, considered her likely to 'stuff her poor babe into her knotting bag when she wanted to play macao, and forget it'.[5]

In the High Great Chamber, the 6th Duke took down 'the old utterly ruined bed called Mary's' (part of the original Best Bed), which had probably been moved there between 1785 and 1792, and installed the late seventeenth-century red velvet bed with embossed metal-thread embroidery from Chatsworth (**95**), together with matching chairs. He sent Christian Bruce's canopy of state to Crace's London workshop 'to be repaired and restored', but found the restored canopy 'too gorgeous for its old place' and placed it in one of the State Rooms at Chatsworth.[6] The Duchess Evelyn, wife of the 9th Duke, later turned it into a state bed for Hardwick, but it is now back in the High Great Chamber.

In the Gallery, the plain eighteenth-century canopy was replaced by the far more showy tester and bedhead from the 1697 state bed at Chatsworth (see **90**), together with 'five richly carved stools [which] were also in that suite of rooms'. The Duke shared with his visitors the thrill felt when 'the tapestry over the door at the North end of this room is lifted and they find themselves in this stupendous and original apartment'. Sadly, this did not prevent him stopping up 'many windows and covering them with spare tapestry', including the fifteenth-century *Hunting Tapestries* now in the Victoria and Albert Museum, in a vain attempt to keep out the cold.

Other parts of the house were made more habitable. The Duke removed the chintz bed from the former Withdrawing Chamber and turned the room into a comfortable library for himself. He used some of the miles of red drugget, bought for the visit to Chatsworth of Queen Victoria and Prince Albert in 1843, to give 'an appearance of warmth and comfort' to the Dining Room, and the dressing-room off the Cut-Velvet Room (**96**) was 'adorned by some very curious needlework of the greatest beauty, said by the old housekeeper at Chatsworth to have come from Londesborough; I found it in that mine over the Chatsworth stables.'[7]

The Duke clearly had a feel for embroidery, and he rescued many of the old pieces scattered about the house, including those in the Drawing Room: 'It was only this year [1844] that the specimens of needlwork … have been produced and framed. Lady Shrewsbury assisting at the Sacrifice of Isaac, and the vengeance of Diana are amusing.' These were the long cushions already described (pp.48–9). Others, including the pair decorated with strawberries and worms (p.63), the Chatsworth Platt (p.52) and the one of red velvet with Bess's arms on a lozenge (p.61), had been turned into screens in the eighteenth century, but some may have survived unaltered. They were, however, framed like pictures with 'the eternal Chatsworth mouldings'.[8]

93 (*below*) and **94** (*below left*) Three valances from a late 18th century bed-set; twill-weave cotton decorated with a Neo-classical design worked with deep pink silk in coral and some satin stitches. The set is trimmed with fringes of knotted linen thread. The detail shows the twill-weave ground and the loosely-plied embroidery silk. (Each valance 32cm deep) Inv. T/19 *NTPL/ John Hammond*

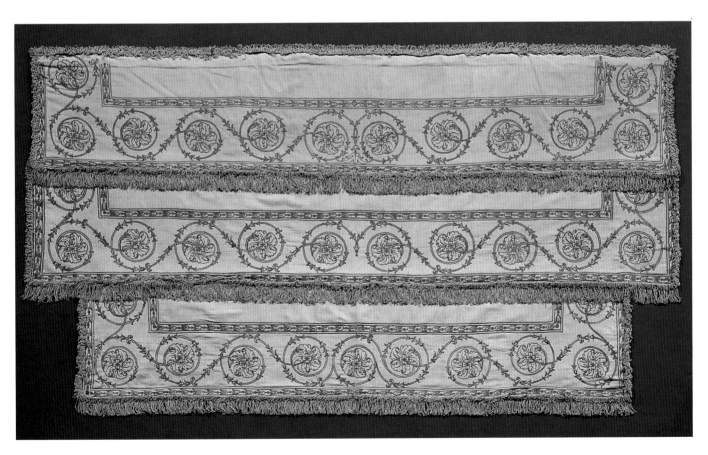

95 The High Great Chamber shown in a watercolour painted by Lake Price *c*.1840. In the window recess is the late 17th-century state bed of embroidered red velvet from Chatsworth; one of the matching stools is also shown (see fig. **86**). Note the painted wall above the windows; the State Drawing Room next door was similarly decorated before it was altered in the 18th century (see p.35). *Devonshire Collection*

The 6th Duke certainly made Hardwick more comfortable. If his aunt, Lady Bessborough, is to be believed, it had not been in a good state at the end of the eighteenth century and she described how 'The little light there is can hardly find its way thro' Ivy and Iron bars that close my casement, and the wind whistles dolefully thro' the crevices and blows about the loose Arras. Nothing can be more gloomy, yet I like it of all things.'[9] As much by spending time there as by his repairs and improvements, the 6th Duke made the house more habitable. By 1845 he considered that 'the offices are good and convenient', and he was proud of the fact that 'though it appears old and unaltered, there has been a great deal done in my time to the house that "Bess of Hardwick" built'. He clearly felt that she would have approved. Certainly, by 1844 his sister Harriet was able to write to him: 'I think of you alone at Hardwick ... a double pleasure to know you are safe and snug at the Hall.'[10] The Duke retired to Hardwick during his final illness, and he died there in January 1858, in Bess's bedchamber, where she had died 250 years before.

The 6th Duke shared his love of Chatsworth and Hardwick with many others, including William and George Cavendish (great-nephews of the 5th Duke). He engineered the marriage of William, who was to succeed him as 7th Duke, to Blanche Howard, of whom he was particularly fond, and whom he hoped would take over the care of the houses.[11] Sadly she died before him, and the widowed 7th Duke preferred to remain at their home, Holker Hall in Lancashire. He and his four children did spend some time in Derbyshire, however, and his daughter Louisa acted as the lady of the house until her marriage to Admiral Egerton in 1865.

Lady Egerton was particularly fond of Hardwick, which her father and then her brother, the 8th Duke (1891-1908), lent to her for the summer months. Towards the end of her life, in 1903, she made a careful record of the alterations undertaken since the 6th Duke's time. They included the destruction of the red velvet bed in the High Great Chamber, 'called Queen Mary's [which] was so entirely devoured by moth that we were obliged to destroy it in 1858 or 1859, [although] every scrap of the curtains which still

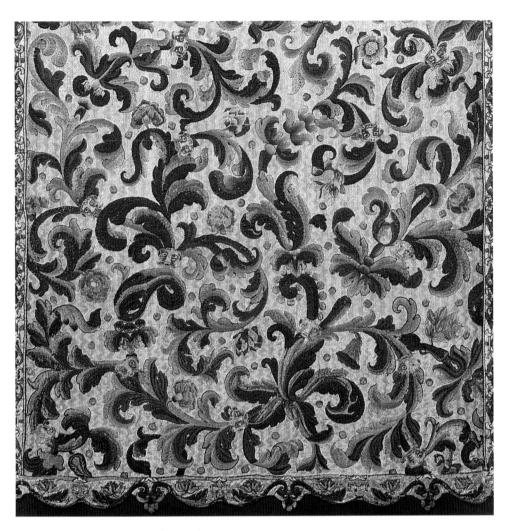

96 Detail of one of the needlework wall-panels of *c.*1700, which the 6th Duke installed in the Dressing Room to the Cut-Velvet Room (fig. **81**). Linen canvas, the pattern worked with wool and a little silk in long-and-short, stem, satin and split stitches, the ground with white silk in flame stitch worked vertically. (Width: 146cm) Inv. T/172 *NTPL/John Hammond*

97 Photograph of the Entrance Hall in 1903. The appliqué hanging of Artemisia can be seen in an unglazed frame at the Gallery end of the room. Banner screens to either side of the fireplace are decorated with needlework motifs including two which relate to those on the Oxburgh hangings, a grotesque mask and floral slips. The informally-positioned furniture ranges in date from the late 17th-to the 19th-century, and the velvet cushions visible here (and in other views of the room) are ornamented with reapplied embroidery. *NT*

98 Miscellaneous furnishings. At the bottom, pieces of needlework from the early 18th century – a chair back and an octagonal table top, both worked with wool and silk on canvas grounds in cross and tent stitches. Above is a valance of red silk damask woven with a design, *Marlborough*, by Owen Jones first registered in 1872, it is lined with glazed wool. One pair and a single heavy red silk tassel from curtain ties, late 19th century. Two case covers of glazed roller-printed cotton from the period 1860s–80s, probably by Thomas Clarkson and Co. of Bannister Hall near Preston, whose printed stamp survives on a related fragment still in the house. Inv. T/338a T/338b, T/44a, T/349, T/352, T/25b, T/349 *NTPL/John Hammond*

99 (*far right*) Compatible pieces from different centuries. A late 16th-century figure of a gentleman mounted on a late 19th-century banner screen; two 19th-century cushions, one with a contemporary top of beaded needlework, the other with a top of 16th-century coloured cutwork. In front are a 19th-century tasselled curtain tie of red and yellow silk, re-used needlework slips of the late 16th century and a border, showing part of its unfaded back, from one of the 17th-century tapestries cut-up in the 19th century to cover bare walls. The background is a length of 19th-century cotton plush. Inv. T/304a, T/301, T/300, T/346, T/297, T/460, T/464 *NTPL/John Hammond*

hung together was made into fire screens, for the Library and Gallery, & also for cushions for chairs in the Entrance Hall'.[12] Most of these have vanished, but some remnants survive in store or are framed on the wall near the foot of the main stairs. Lady Egerton followed the 6th Duke's example in framing more of the embroideries, but she also began to put right his savage treatment of the tapestries by instituting a programme of restoration under the supervision of Miss Gemmel of the South Kensington Museum (now the Victoria and Albert) – 'one piece alone took 8 ladies fourteen months to repair'. This task was continued by her sister-in-law, the Duchess Evelyn, whose painstaking work in piecing together fragments gathered from throughout the house is described by her daughter Lady Maud Baillie in an account of life at Hardwick published in the 1996 guidebook.

Lady Egerton was also responsible for moving *The Virtues* hangings down to the Hall. She did this 'to make it more "liveable"', and the unglazed screens were placed under the Gallery (**97**) where, according to the Duchess Evelyn, 'every time the doors were opened scraps of brocade fell off'.[13] The hangings by the door were subsequently moved by Duchess Evelyn to the Chapel Landing and they and the remaining hangings in the Hall were glazed. Photographs taken of the Hall in Lady Egerton's time give some idea of the quantity of furniture then in the house. This was in keeping with the deliberately informal look of late Victorian and Edwardian interiors, in which clusters of furniture were spread across a room, providing several points of focus and designed to accommodate the differing needs of a large house party.

Textiles played a prominent role in such interiors; there were carpets and rugs, draped curtains and upholstered furniture, a variety of loose covers, antimacassars, cushions and pole-screens. The materials once more included velvets and plush, silk damask, the nineteenth-century version of chintz, embroidery and needlework, as well as elaborate fringes and tassels (98). There was at Hardwick an amazing mix of furniture and furnishings from different houses and different periods (see 86), but the pole-screen made from a pair of Elizabethan long cushions (see 59), and others cut from a late seventeenth-century state bed, not to mention the sixteenth-century cushions of coloured cutwork, no doubt looked comfortably at home with the Victorian beadwork and draperies of plush (99). Although lacking the formality of the original State Rooms, and having an increased density of furniture, Hardwick in about 1900 was probably closer in spirit and general ambience to the Hardwick of 1601 than at any intermediate point. At both times the interior was dominated by textiles and there was a mix of furniture and of periods, but, whereas Bess had drawn on a smaller number of houses and a period of some sixty years, by 1900 the number of houses was greater and the time-span was more than three hundred years.

Change did not stop in 1900 any more than it had in 1600; the sale of Devonshire House in 1920 resulted in another influx of furniture to Derbyshire, and the problem of keeping tabs on it all was explained by Duchess Evelyn in an update of the 6th Duke's *Handbook*, which she wrote in 1924 for her daughter-in-law Lady Mary Cecil, wife of the future 10th Duke. She had, for example, gathered together two sets of eighteenth-century furniture scattered between the Footmen's Waiting Room at Chatsworth, the Cook's Room at Devonshire House and the Housekeeper's Room at Hardwick, where a sofa from one of the sets was still in the State Bedroom. She had many similar stories to tell both to her daughter-in-law and later to the National Trust, for whom she described some of the changes made at Hardwick, following the same route through the house as the compilers of the 1601 inventory.[14]

Duchess Evelyn gave much time to working out what alterations had taken place since 1601 and, where she could, she returned furniture and furnishings to their original setting. She reintroduced rush matting, 'made by two old ladies at Brimington', into the State Rooms, where she also installed several nineteenth-century Persian carpets. She personally mended and pieced together the damaged tapestries, replacing large missing sections with painted canvas, as can be seen in the borders of one of the *Prodigal Son* tapestries in the Cut-Velvet Room. It was at her instigation that the blocked windows in the Gallery were reopened and the fifteenth-century *Hunting Tapestries* were sent away to be put back together, although then 'no place could be found large enough to hold them'. Before the hangings of *The Virtues* were glazed, she had them repaired by members of the Decorative Needlework Society, who were a little heavy-handed. She noted that 'the taffeta used for the faces had quite worn off so they put a little tempera on the canvas, rather too much in some cases'. She herself remounted many of the needlework slips on brown velvet, chosen to match a badly dyed black velvet of the nineteenth century, which had turned brown. Some of it can be seen on the canopy in the High Great Chamber.

This survey of the house and its furnishings must finish, however, as do all the inventories of the house, with a brief look at the linen, which did not decline in importance or value through the centuries (100). In 1764 the list of linen at Chatsworth covered five and a half foolscap pages, that at Hardwick fewer than two, a clear indication that the house was not lived in on a regular basis. It was relatively poorly equipped, with nine large and ten small diaper cloths and two damask ones. Another twenty-six small cloths had been made from old ones – including three from Chatsworth that had been cut down. The bed linen included eleven calico sheets, thirteen pairs of holland sheets 'for upper servants', and fourteen coarse sheets. Interestingly, there were another '35 pair of coarse sheets of Margery's spining'. The only yardage lengths were 33 yards of coarse linen and 'A Piece of Harden for Venison sheets 25 yards' – an indication of Hardwick's use as a hunting-lodge. There was a small quantity of linen for general domestic purposes, including 'Chamber Stool Covers' for the close stools still used in the house, and also ten rubbers, a term wider than, but including, the modern duster. At Chatsworth, however, there were many more, separately marked for their particular purpose and counted by the dozen: 1 for the Store Room, 2 for the Nursery, 3 for the Confectioner, 3 for the Housemaids, 5 for the Pantry, 1 for the Bowls, 2 for the Kitchen.

The altered status of Hardwick by 1782 is clearly demonstrated by the increased quantity of linen; some of the 1764 linen was still there, including the calico sheets, which

100 (*right*) Section of the linen cupboard showing the ends of rolled aprons, piles of damask table napkins in sets of up to 14 dozen, and damask table cloths stored according to size. Those at the front are marked in red silk with a coronet, H for Hardwick, and a number indicating the banqueting table to which they belonged. *NTPL/Nadia MacKenzie*

101 (*far right*) Woollen blankets in store in the Housekeeper's Room. Some on the two lower shelves are stitched in the corners with large 'roses' worked with coloured wools; although more common in the 18th century, they continued to be made into the mid-19th century. On the two upper shelves are blankets of the later 19th- and early 20th-centuries, including some from the 1870s which are dated and marked with a coronet and DD, for the Duke of Devonshire. *NTPL/Nadia MacKenzie*

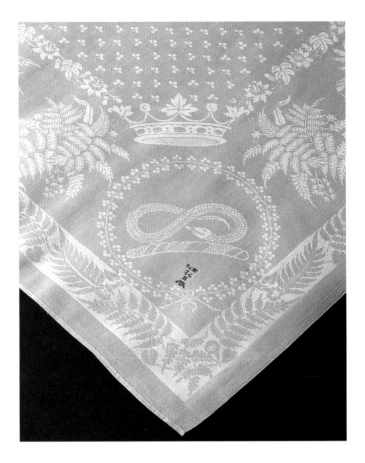

102 Corner of a linen damask napkin woven with a coronet and the Cavendish snake. Marked in blue silk with a coronet, an H for Hardwick, the number 27 and the date 1872. Part of a large set woven by James Coulson and Co. for the visit of the Prince and Princess of Wales. Inv. T/470
NTPL/John Hammond

were now 'used as counterpanes occasionally'. But much more bed and table linen was described as 'new' or 'nearly new'. The miscellaneous items had increased to encompass 16 pudding bags, 102 glass-cloths, 3 cloths used in mangling, 3 folding-cloths and 51 new kitchen dusters; there were no longer any rubbers. There were also 11 pairs of homespun sheets and 4 yards of 'Home-made Sheeting', an indication that Margery had a successor.

By 1811, the linen had increased both in quantity and quality, and this time the inventory clerks measured it all. The largest damask table cloths measured 5 × 2½ yards and the smallest 2¼ × 1¾ yards. There were 66 damask cloths, 13 of diaper, 31 of huckaback, plus another 20 for the Servants' Hall. There was also a substantial quantity of yardage fabric, including 14½ yards of fine Irish diaper. During the 6th Duke's time, the Housekeeper's Room was moved and the new one equipped with presses for the storage of bed linen and blankets (**101**). Other cupboards were installed outside the Pantry for the table linen (**100**) and both were full when the house was passed to the National Trust in 1959. Among the table linen was a fine set of damask specially woven by the Irish firm of James Coulson & Co. for the visit of the Prince and Princess of Wales in 1872 (**102**). Lady Frederick Cavendish, the wife of the 8th Duke's brother, described the preparation: 'All is being pondered and prearranged in true deliberate Cavendish style; and I quite expect that when once the whole machine is given a shove on Tuesday, off it will go everything in its proper place, from the Duke to the scullery-maid.'[15] The building and running of a great house was a great undertaking.

NOTES

INTRODUCTION

1. PRO, II/111/ff.188-92. There is a second copy in the Chatsworth Archive.
2. Durant (1977), Appendix II, Durant and Riden (1984), p.lvi. The value of the textiles has been calculated from the known costs of such items as tapestries and carpets, the recorded prices of yardage fabric and trimmings, and bills relating to a set of embroidered bed hangings in the Talbot papers.

CHAPTER ONE

1. Elizabeth Hardwick, born c.1527, had been married at the age of 15, probably in May 1543, to the even younger Robert Barley, who died in December 1544.
2. Sixteenth-century money cannot meaningfully be translated into twentieth-century values, but comparative costs will be given where possible. See Appendix for details of sixteenth-century coinage.
3. Hunter (1869), p.107.
4. Hard. MS 143/2, from which all the following quotations are taken. One of Bess's corrections is given in brackets {}. For details of measurements in use in the sixteenth and seventeenth centuries see Appendix.
5. Most of the surviving account books are in the Archive at Chatsworth, but the earliest book and one kept by Bess's London Steward between 1589 and 1592 are in the Folger Shakespeare Library, Washington (MSS X.d.485 and V.b.308).
6. Folger, MS X.d.485 (n.p.). The total cost of the linen for sheets should be lxˢ not liiˢ. See Appendix for Latin numerals and Glossary for ells.
7. CSP, Scots, VIII, p.312.
8. Hard. MS 1, f.4r; Folger, MS X.d.486 (n.p.).
9. Hunter, 'Expenses' (1828), p.149.
10. Hard. MS 143/6. The date is not given, but it is likely to have been about 1562-3.
11. There are seventeenth-century references to mixed sets of heroes drawn from classical and Old Testament sources, as well as evidence that 'sets' were completed with near-matching pieces. I am grateful to Wendy Hefford for this information.
12. Hard. MS 278/1. Provision was made for marriages with other of the children should any of the main parties die.
13. Shrewsbury owned seven main houses: Sheffield Castle and Manor,

Rufford Abbey, Welbeck Abbey, Wingfield Manor, Worksop Manor, Buxton Hall, plus one house in the City of London and one at Chelsea. He also rented Tutbury Castle from the Crown.
14. See Durant (1977), pp.113-14.
15. Girouard (1973), pp.1668-77.
16. Hard. MS 4, f.47v.
17. CSP, Scots, IV, p.100.
18. Hunter (1869), pp.115-16.
19. For details of the deed of gift see Durant (1977), pp.77-9.
20. Letter of 20 August 1584 from the Earl of Shrewsbury to the Earl of Leicester, HMC, Longleat, vol. V Talbot Papers, p.52.
21. David Durant has calculated that Mary was moved 46 times, with her retainers and all their baggage. Durant (1977), p.73.
22. Inventory of Sheffield Castle, 1582, transcribed in the *British Archaeological Journal*, vol.30, 1874, pp.251-63.
23. HMC, Hatfield, Salisbury Papers, III, pp.158-61.
24. There is no doubt that Mary and her retinue were a severe drain on the Earl's resources. His complaints were continual until Mary was removed from his charge in 1584, when Sir Ralph Sadler stated that 'She hath no stuff of her own, neither hangings, bedding, plate, napery, kitchen vessels, nor anything else, but occupieth all my Lord's; and ... as for the Queen's Majesty's [Elizabeth's] stuff which was sent to this Queen [in 1568] it is told me that there in a manner nothing of it serviceable, save the hangings and a chair or two, but it is worn and spent besides much of the Earl's stuff that is also wasted, as his officers say.' (CSP, Sadler, III, p.194).
25. HMC, Hatfield, Salisbury Papers, III, pp.158-61. In a second copy of Shrewsbury's list, additional textile items, including counterpoints, square carpets, window cloths, 'a long carpet made all of silk', Turkish carpets, hangings and tapestries, have all been struck out, presumably before the list was submitted to Bess. *Ibid.*, p.158.
26 HMC, Various Papers 7, 1914, p.263.

CHAPTER TWO

1. For details of Bess's finances during and after the quarrel, see Durant (1977), pp.152, 155, 157.
2. Arbella was the great-grand-daughter of Margaret Tudor, the sister of Henry VIII, and her second husband, the Earl of Angus. Mary Queen of Scots was the granddaughter of Margaret and her first husband,

James IV of Scotland. Had Arbella been a boy, it is possible that Queen Elizabeth would have declared the male English child her heir, to the exclusion Mary's son, James VI of Scotland. By the time the New Hall was completed, relations between Bess and Arbella were very strained.
3. J. Denucé (1931). I am grateful to Wendy Hefford for this reference.
4. Letter to Bess, 13 October 1575, Hunter (1869), p.114. The italics are Gilbert Talbot's.
5. Hard. MSS. 6 and 7. See Durant and Riden (1980 and 1984).
6. Copies exist in the Chatsworth Archive and in the PRO, Prob. II/111, ff.193-208. The Hardwick inventory is published in *Furniture History*, VII, 1971.
7. The rooms at Chatsworth are described in the 1601 inventory; Bess's Withdrawing Chamber had 'french pannell markentree', perhaps denoting the presence of French workmen, as well as the influence of French designs. French and Flemish workmen were recorded at several other houses. (Girouard (1983), pp.14-16).
8. Durrant and Riden (1984), p.lxvi.
9. Hard. MS 7, f.94r and v.
10. Hard. MS 8, f.63r.
11. Batho, P. f.977.
12. Thornton (1978), p.358 n.110. John Waterer has identified only two makers of gilt leather working in London around 1600, although he found it 'hardly credible that gilt leather, this highly fashionable material which was widely admired, was not produced in England well before 1600.' (Waterer (1971), pp.61-2).
13. Batho, F. f.157.
14. Hard. MS. 7. f.28v.
15. Hard. MS. 8, ff.29v and 30r.
16. Hard. MS. 7, ff.18r, 21v, 28v.
17. Folger, MS. V.b.308 (n.p.), margin note, 20 July, 21 October 1591.
18. Duchess Evelyn gives two different dates for its acquisition, 1587 and 1597, but it does not appear in the surviving records.
19. Sir William Pickering was a diplomat and courtier who died in January 1574/75. Bess may have known him from her time at Court between Cavendish's death and her marriage to St Loe, when Sir William was briefly regarded as a suitor to Queen Elizabeth. He was a close friend of Cecil (later Lord Burghley) and was probably well known to Lord Shrewsbury.
20. Wendy Hefford suggests that Bess may have received on approval the two pieces (one with and one without gold) which she decided to buy on 6

March 1592, although she completed the set with the cheaper silk-enhanced pieces. One was ready by 20 April, but she had to wait until 10 July for the fourth.
21. HMC, Hatfield, Salisbury Papers, IV, p.138.
22. Four 'peses of Tapestre off the story of Prodygus' were listed in the Chatsworth inventory of 1562 (Hard. MS 143/6) but only three were at Hardwick in 1601. The fourth must already have been transferred to Bess's youngest son, Charles Cavendish, since it was later recorded at Welbeck, the home of his descendants.
23. The hangings in Jacob's Chamber are not named in the inventory but Old Bromley was paid for panelling 'the Chamber weare the story of Jacobe hangeth.' in December 1596. (Hard. MS 7, f.225v).
24. Digby (1980), nos. 2-5. The depths of the four remaining damaged and rejoined pieces vary from 13′ 4″ to 14′ 6″, those recorded in 1601 were all 15′ 6″ deep.
25 There were 78 pieces of tapestry in 1601; today there are 104 plus several large fragments. I am grateful to John Entwhistle for providing me with details of those now in the house and for helping me to look at the stored pieces.
26. HMC, Hatfield, Salisbury Papers, IV, p.358.
27. Lodge (1838), vol. II, p.582n. By 1614, following the growth of direct trade with the Levant, prices had dropped and William Sexton, the London agent for the Manvers family, paid £18 6s for a large Turkish carpet bought 'against the kings coming', so presumably of good quality.
28. 1588 inventory of Kenilworth Castle, transcribed in Halliwell (1854), p.146.
29. King and Sylvester (1983), pp.26 and 37; Bennet and Franses, pp.109-10. I am grateful to Jennifer Wearden for the information on coats of arms in sixteenth-century oriental carpets; it is also possible that the clerks failed to distinguish between Turkish and other oriental carpets.
30. In addition to Lord Leicester's Norwich carpet, Peter Thornton cites several late sixteenth-century examples (see Thornton (1983), p.110, n.33).
31. Hard. MS 7, f.42v.
32. A journal of their travels was kept by Henry's servant, Fox; it is published in *Camden Miscellany XVII*. Henry had also travelled in Italy between 1569 and 1571, when he visited Venice, the then centre of the Levant trade. He was only about twenty, however, and interested in matters other than trade.

33. Evidence that Lord Shrewsbury bought goods on behalf of his wife, for which she paid, is provided by correspondence between him and his London Steward and by details of a cargo brought back from Rouen in 1575. Lambeth, MS 697; Lodge (1838), vol. II, pp.68-73.

34. Lambeth, MS 695, f.695; see also Allgrove (1988), pp.38-41.

35. Hard. MS 7, ff.11v, 27r; MS 8. f.97r.

36. Hard. MS 8, f.63v; Hard. MS 7, ff.24v, 25v.

37. Hard. MS 7, ff.24v, 31r.

38. Hard. MS 8, f.70r.

39. Hard. MS 7, f.24v; MS. 8, f.102r.

40. Hard. MS. 143/6.

41. Folger, MS.V.b.308.

42. Fustian was originally made in England of wool and cotton.

43. Hard. MS 8, ff.32v, 40r, 86v.

44. Batho, F. f.150 seq. A 'piece' was a length of fabric as it came off the loom. Different fabrics were woven in pieces of different standard lengths. The 1582 inventory is transcribed in *The British Archaeological Journal*, 30, 1874, pp.251-63.

45. Hard. MS 8, f.63v.

46. Hard. MS 7, ff.11v, 12v, 30r; MS 8, f.48v.

47. Hard. MS 1, f.3.

48. Hard. MS 8, f.52v.

49. Hard. MS 8, ff.70r and v, 73v, 74r.

50. Lambeth, MS 702, f.69; MS 700, f.61; MS 694, f.132. The curtains and headpiece were cheaper because of 'the owter pte of bothe [great curtains] beinge plaine & unwrought'.

51. I am grateful to Lisa Monnas for her advice on the sixteenth-century meaning of these terms.

52. Hard. MS 7, f.30r.

53. Hard. MS 7, ff.11v, 27v. The damask was not described as silk, but had it been of linen, it would have been bought from a linen draper, not a mercer.

54. Hard. MS 7, ff.9r, 17r, 18r, 22r, 24v; MS 8, ff.48v, 126v.

55. Hard. MS 7, f.21r – it cost 10s a yd. This purchase may, however, have been for the liveries of Bess's servants, which were of blue cloth.

56. Lodge (1838), vol. II, pp.68-73.

57. Hard. MS 7, f.85r; MS 8, f.76v.

58. Hard MS 8, ff.76v-77r. Sheldon's position in the household is not known, although he clearly was responsible for the table linen used in the Hall.

59. Hard MS 7, ff.22r, 28v; MS 7, f.31r.

60. The Maids' Room at Chatsworth was fitted with wooden presses that may have held the fine linen as well as Bess's clothes.

61. The present small overmantel was brought from Chatsworth and installed when the ceiling was lowered in the eighteenth century.

62. This is supported by the relatively unfaded condition of the Abraham tapestries despite their subsequent use at Chatsworth and elsewhere at Hardwick.

63. When Queen Elizabeth was dying she initially refused to be moved from the pile of cushions on which she reclined.

64. There were three pictures relating to Mary Queen of Scots: one of her alone, a double portrait of her with her second husband Darnley, and a third of her parents. The others showed the Earl of Leicester, William St Loe, Bess's daughter Mary, as Countess of Shrewsbury, and her youngest son Charles Cavendish and his first wife Margaret Kitson.

65. While in London in 1591-2, she provided herself with a substantial store of wool, silk and linen fabric. Hard. MS 7, *passim*.

66. Several gift rolls have survived and are listed in Arnold (1988), p.243.

67. Hard. MS 7, ff.16r, 17v.

68. The portrait is something of a puzzle; if it is the one that was transported from London in the summer of 1599 (Hard. MS 8, f.56v), the payment in March 1600/01 (Hard. MS 8, f.118) cannot relate to it. It is also more likely that the Queen is shown wearing a stained or painted petticoat, rather than an embroidered one. This still suggests a link with Bess, however, since several of her furnishings combine the two techniques, while the motifs relate to those embroidered by Bess and the Queen of Scots on the Oxburgh Hangings.

69. The portraits were of Queen Elizabeth, the Earl of Shrewsbury, Lord Burghley, the Countess of Lennox, her son Charles, who married Bess's daughter Elizabeth, and their daughter Arbella. In addition, there were portraits of Bess, her second husband Sir William Cavendish, his father Thomas Cavendish, his and Bess's son William Cavendish and their grandson the younger William. Despite her Protestant affiliations, Bess had a number of paintings of the Virgin, suggesting a degree of tolerance that encompassed pre-Reformation saints and traditions.

70. Hard. MS 8, f.104r.

71. Hard. MS 8, ff.109v, 150r; Durant (1977), p.185.

72. Bess's granddaughter, Arbella Stuart, was originally left an agate cup, a sable fur with a jewelled clasp and }other jewels, but this bequest was rescinded when Arbella was cut out of the will in 1603, and not restored in 1607 when she was partially written back in.

73. HMC, Longleat, V, Dudley Papers, p.33.

CHAPTER THREE

1. Lodge (1838), vol. II, p.73. In 1577 more silk thread was acquired from France through Mary Queen of Scots.

2. Lord Shrewsbury bitterly complained that 'no man of understanding can think that I and my wife wittingly should be glad of such tedious hourly attendance to the want of our own liberties' (Letter to Sir William Cecil, 8 April 1569, CSP, Dom. II, p.638).

3. Gage (1822), p.191. One of the Kitson daughters, Margaret, was to be the first wife of Bess's youngest son Charles Cavendish.

4. Hard. MS 8, f.61v. Tasker was paid 53s 8d.

5. Folger, MS X.d.486, *passim*.

6. Folger, MS X.d.486, for Angell; Hard. MS 4, f.40 for Barnet.

7. Hard MS 8, ff.79v, 97r, 116v, 119r. His status within the household is not entirely clear, however, since he was also given 30s 3d to buy a livery coat in 1590 (Hard. MS 8, f.90) and there is evidence that, like Balechouse and other of Bess's long-term favoured servants, she awarded him leases on land or property. He paid rents on different places in 1598 and 1601 (Hard. MS 9, f.24v; 143/11v).

8. The term upholsterer had a much wider meaning before the late nineteenth century. In 1551, the overlap between embroidery and upholstery was dealt with in the Statutes of the Parisian Guild of Embroiderers (De Farcy (1890), vol. I, p.24).

9. MS 8, ff.28v, 44v; f.45r, f.99r. Franke's wife also appears in William Cavendish's accounts from 1608 onwards.

10. In March 1598/9 Bess paid 16s for a pound of black London silk and 26s 8d for a pound of black Spanish silk (Hard. MS 8, f.47r).

11. Hard. MS 8, f.54r.

12. Thompson(1815), p.235.

13. Nichols (1823), vol. III, p.554; Williams (1959), p.233; HMC, Hatfield, Salisbury Papers, XII, pp.593-6.

14. MS 8, f.138. The canvas was woven to a standard width for cushions.

15. Many such pieces survive in Scotland and England, and Margaret Swain has argued that their proven dependence on a mix of widely available printed sources makes it likely that they were worked there (see Swain (1970), pp.27-9).

16. C. L. Kingsford, 'The Inventory of Leicester House', in *Archaeologia*, 73, 1922-3, p.40.

17. They were: Calvin's *Sermons upon the Booke of Job* (1574), 'the resolution' – probably *A Briefe Resolution of a Right Religion* by C.S. (1590), *A Commentarie upon the Proverbes of Solomon*, of which several versions existed, 'a Book of meditations and too other books Covered with black velvet'.

18. Letter to Sir Henry Brounker, *c.* 7 March 1602/3. Steen (1994), pp.156-7.

19. Wells-Cole (1997), chapter 15.

20. Mary Markham's undated letter was written in about 1600 (Batho, O, f.40). In 1600 another painter, called Woodham, was working at Hardwick with John Balechouse and his son (Hard. MS 8, f.93v).

21. Digby (1963), p.101.

22. Letter written by Nicholas White to Sir William Cecil on 26 February 1568/9. HMC, Hatfield, Salisbury Papers, I, p.400.

23. This has been identified by Anthony Wells-Cole as having been based on a tiny scene within an elaborate cartouche engraved by Pieter van der Heyden after Jacob Floris, published in Antwerp in 1566. Wells-Cole (1997), p.257.

24. The badly damaged table carpet is being conserved by Ksynia Marko, who estimates its original size as about 4m × 2.5m.

25. Nevinson, 'Elizabethan Herbarium', (1975-6).

26. Hard. MS 7, f.53v.

27. V & A, T.47-54-1972. The manuscript survives with eight canvas panels worked with needlework slips and a wreath containing the arms of Fitzwilliam impaling Sydney.

28. Swain (1973), pp.56 and 91.

29. The source was first identified by Arthur G. Credland in 'The Hunting Crossbow in England', (1987), pp.40-46.

30. She is known to have bought fabric and sewing silks from France and she certainly tried, although it is not known with what success, to purchase an elaborate bed for the Earl and Countess of Shrewsbury.

31. Several paintings of Lucretia are recorded in the 1547 inventory of the effects of Henry VIII, a full transcript of which is to be published by The Society of Antiquaries of London in association with Harvey Miller Publishers, 1998-9, together with two volumes of explanatory essays.

32. Nos. 12, 881 and 13023 in the inventory of King Henry VIII; Levey (1998/9).

33. Lodge (1838), vol. II, p.33; letter of 10 August 1573.

34. Swain (1973), *passim*.

35. CSP, Scots. II, p.632; Strickland, I, p.224. Bastian remained with Mary throughout her imprisonment.

36. Wells-Cole (1997), p.257-60.

37. Walpole, *Journals* (ed. Toynbee, 1927-9), p.30.

38. Anthony Wells-Cole suggests that he may have been responsible for the painting of Ulysses returning to Penelope. Wells-Cole (1997), p.288.

39. Hard. MS 8, f.82

40. Hard. MS 7, ff.136v, 138r.

CHAPTER FOUR

1. He invested in the Company the considerable sum of about £1,000 a year over a period of some 15 years. (Stone (1965), p.372).

2. Mark Girouard has suggested that it was William who introduced decorative plaster work in the Gallery and elsewhere and converted one of the turrets into a Banquet; both are likely to have had Bess's approval.

3. Hard. MS 29, f.84. Halifax cloth

was probably a heavy woollen fabric, perhaps a double cloth.

4. Hard. MS 27. In the two following years repairs were carried out at Hardwick and Chatsworth and £80 was spent on the Derby almshouses. The manuscript is calendared as dating from the time of the 2nd Earl and Christian Bruce, but it relates mainly to the 1st Earl. Entries include £625 and £82 06s 03d for 'Adventures to the East Indies' and 'Somers Islands' respectively.

5. Hard. MS 26. The inventory may have been taken when the house in Aldersgate was changed for a larger house, with a big garden, in Bishopsgate. Both are shown on Ogilby's and Morgan's 1675 map of the City of London.

6. Pomfret (1685), pp.26 and 33.

7. Pomfret (1685), p.35.

8. Hard. MS 30A.

9. Braids and tapes were often sold not by the yard, but in packets containing standard lengths.

10. Christian Bruce had a second couch bed made with ten matching chairs for the low drawing chamber at Leicester Abbey, some of which may have ended up at Hardwick.

11. Quoted in Montgomery (1984), p.372. Like scarlet, the name did not necessarily denote the colour.

12. There are fragments of appliqué and couched thread on the squab of her couch, but they appear to date from later than the seventeenth century.

13. Hard. MS 26.

14. A total of 256 yards of diaper was purchased for £22 10s 4d, plus 108 ells of linen for £10 13s, 10 ells of Gentishe (from Ghent) for £2 8s 4d, and, finally, 24 ells of damask for £1 10s – interestingly the damask was cheaper than the diaper.

15. Pomfret (1685), p.41.

16. Hard. MS 14.

17. The very decayed cushions are now in store.

18. Hard. MS 143/25.

19. Quoted in Pearson (1983), p.45.

20. While the new Piccadilly house was being built, he rented Montacute House from the Earl of Bedford. Unfortunately, just as he was about to leave in January 1685/6, the house caught fire and 'my Lord Devonshire's loss in pictures, hangings and other furniture is very considerable'. Ellis (1827), vol. IV, pp.89-90.

21. Beard and Westman '(1993), pp.515-25.

22. The movement and installation at Hardwick of panelling from Chatsworth is recorded in 1690 (Girouard (1973), p.1671). Bishop White Kennett refers in his *Memoires of the Family of Cavendish* (1708) to 'Her Chamber & Rooms of State, with her Arms and othe Ensigns still remaining at Hardwick', p.5. Some panelling from the Old Hall seems also to have been moved across.

23. 1778. Quoted in Stone (1984), p.253.

24. Walpole, *Journals* (ed. Toynbee, 1927-8) p.28.

25. Chatsworth had been open on request to the Housekeeper since its rebuilding and Monday was to become a formal open day from the time of the 4th Duke. Hardwick could also be inspected on application to its Housekeeper.

26. Walpole, Letter to George Montague, 1 September 1760, *Letters*, IV, p.423. and Walpole, *Journals*, (ed. Toynbee, 1927-8) p.30.

27. Chatsworth Archive.

28. The room was sparsely furnished, although the inlaid table and possibly three of the original stools were still there. It suggests, however, that the Duke had died before the room could be fitted out for its new purpose.

29. Walpole's *Journals* (ed. Toynbee, 1927-8) p.30 and *Letters* (ed. Toynbee, 1904), pp.423-4. His descriptions make it possible to identify several of the 1601 furnishings.

30. Walpole, *Journals* (ed. Toynbee 1927-8), p.28.

31. One of them was probably that recorded in 1764 in the room next to Her Grace's Dressing Room at Chatsworth.

32. Kennett (1708), p.5. It is unlikely. that Walpole would have described the bed he saw in 1760 as 'modern' without additional comment had it incorporated parts of the best bed. Nor is Grimm's bed shown to be 'worked' in the usual sense of being decorated with an all-over pattern in white linen or in coloured silks or crewel wools.

33. Several complete 'washing beds' of printed cotton were in the Wardrobe – presumably for summer use. The inventory was taken in December.

34. Bessborough (1955), p.113. 'Bess' refers to Lady Elizabeth Foster, friend of Georgiana, mistress of the 5th Duke and later his second wife.

35. Torrington (ed. Andrews, 1938), vol. III, pp.30-8.

36. The Old Hall continued to be used for over-spill accommodation until the 6th Duke built the present Servants' Wing in the nineteenth century.

37. A cut-velvet bed moved from elsewhere in the house was in the Leicester Room at Chatsworth by 1792.

38. Letter to Sir Henry Brounker, quoted in Steen (1994), pp.149-54.

39. Quoted in Cornforth (1995), p.39.

40. Quoted in Steen (1994), p.151.

41. Devonshire (1845), p.51.

42. Plain wooden floors nonetheless remained in even the grandest houses well into the second half of the century, as portraits and inventories show.

43. Devonshire (1845), p.82.

CHAPTER FIVE

1. Bessborough (1940), pp.192 and 197.

2. Devonshire (1845), p.185.

3. This is probably the bed described as new in the 1764 inventory of Chatsworth.

4. Devonshire (1845), pp.187, 212, 216.

5. Walpole, *Letters* (ed. Toynbee, 1904), p.27.

6. Devonshire (1845), pp.187, 189, 133.

7. Devonshire (1845), pp.208, 212.

8. Devonshire (1845), p.208. The frames were made from moulding of about 1700 that the Duke had stripped out of the Queen of Scots Apartment at Chatsworth.

9. Bessborough (1940), p.118.

10. Quoted in Leverson-Gower (1940), vol. II, p.386.

11. She was the daughter of his sister Georgiana, Lady Carlisle.

12. Lady Egerton's 'Notes on the Sixth Duke's Handbook of . . . Hardwick' (1903) are in the Chatsworth Archive.

13. Duchess Evelyn's 'Notes on Hardwick', p.109. The notes were written as a supplement to the 1601 inventory in 1946. Duchess Evelyn also annotated Lady Egerton's notes, and towards the end of her life recorded both further information about her own activities and pieces of information collected from various sources; at the end of the book she described her approach to the conservation of the textiles. This last manuscript is at Hardwick, the earlier notebooks are in the Archive at Chatsworth, together with her update of the 6th Duke's *Handbook*.

14. *Ibid.*

15. Barley (1927) vol. II, p.143.

BIBLIOGRAPHY

Manuscript Collections

Chatsworth House:
  Hardwick MSS 1, 2, 3, 4, 5, 6, 7, 8, 9,
    10A & B, 14, 15, 16, 17, 19, 23, 24,
    26, 27, 29, 30A, 34, 66, 143(2), (6)
    & (17).
  Inventories of Chatsworth and
    Hardwick made in 1764, 1792 and
    1811.
  Lady Egerton, *Notes on the Sixth
    Duke's Handbook of Chatsworth and
    Hardwick*, 1903.
  Evelyn, Duchess of Devonshire,
    Notes on the 6th Duke's Handbook,
    1924.
  Evelyn, Duchess of Devonshire,
    *Notes on Hardwick following the 1601
    Inventory*, 1946.

Hardwick:
  Evelyn, Duchess of Devonshire,
    Miscellaneous notes on Hardwick,
    c.1960.

Folger Shakespeare Library,
Washington, U.S.A.:
  X.d. 486 The earliest account book,
    1548-1550.
  V.b. 308 Richard Whaley's London
    account book, September
    1589-July 1592.
  X.d. 428 Cavendish/Talbot letters.

Public Record Office:
  Probate II/111/ff.188-208. Bess's
    will and the 1601 inventories of
    Chatsworth and the two Halls at
    Hardwick.

Lambeth Palace Library:
  Talbot Papers MSS 494, 694, 695,
    700, 704, 705, 706, 707, 708, 709.

Calendared Papers

Public Record Office:
  State Papers Domestic.
  State Papers Scottish.
  Sadler Papers and Letters.

Historical Manuscript Commission:
  Bath, Longleat, vol. V, Talbot,
    Dudley and Devereux Papers.
  Pepys, Magdalene College,
    Cambridge, vol. I.
  Rutland, Belvoir, vols. I-III.
  Salisbury, Hatfield, vols. I-IV.
  Various Papers 7, (1914).

Derbyshire Archaeological Society
Record Series:
  Bill, E. B. W., (ed.), *The Shrewsbury
    Papers at Lambeth Palace Library*,
    1965.
  Batho, G. R., (ed.), *A Calendar of the
    Talbot papers in the College of Arms*,
    1968.

Books and Periodicals

Allgrove McDowell, Joan, 'The
  Textiles at Hardwick Hall', (2 parts)
  Hali Magazine, nos. 39 and 40, 1988.
Arnold, Janet, *Queen Elizabeth's
  Wardrobe Unlock'd*, W. S. Maney &
  Son, 1988.
Barley, John, (ed.), *The Diary of Lady
  Frederick Cavendish*, (2 vols.) Richard
  Bentley & Son, 1927.
Beard, G. and Westman, A., 'A French
  Upholsterer in England: Francis
  Lapierre, 1653-1714', *The Burlington
  Magazine*, vol. CXXXV, 1993.
Bennet, Ian, and Franses, Michael,
  'The Early European and Oriental
  Carpets at Boughton', in *Boughton
  House: The English Versailles*, ed.
  Tessa Murdoch, Faber &
  Faber/Christies, 1992.
Bessborough, Earl of, *Lady Bessborough
  and her Family Circle*, 1940.
Bessborough, Earl of, (ed.), *Georgiana;
  Extracts from the Correspondence of
  Georgiana, Duchess of Devonshire*, 1955.
Bickley, Francis, *The Cavendish Family*,
  Constable, 1911.
Boynton, Lindsay, and Thornton,
  Peter, 'The Hardwick Inventory',
  Furniture History, vol. VII, 1971.
Bradley, E. T., *A Life of the Lady
  Arabella Stuart*, (2 vols.) 1889.
Campbell, Thomas, 'Tapestry Quality
  in Tudor England: Problems of
  Terminology,' in *Studies in the
  Decorative Arts*, vol. III, no.1,
  Fall-Winter 1995-6.
Clabburn, Pamela, *Furnishing Textiles*,
  National Trust, 1988.
Collins, Arthur, *Historical Collections of
  the Noble Families of Cavendish, etc.*,
  1752.
Cooper, Elizabeth, *The Life and Letters
  of Lady Arabella Stuart*, (2 vols.)
  Hurst & Blackett, 1866.
Cornforth, John, 'Hardwick Hall,
  Derbyshire', *Country Life*, 24 August,
  1995.
Credland, Arthur, 'The Hunting
  Crossbow in England', *The Journal of
  the Society of Archer-Antiquarians*, vol.
  30, 1987.
De Farcy, Louis, *La Broderie du xj' siècle
  jusqu'à nos jours*, (3 vols.) 1890-1900.
Denucé, J., 'Art-Export in the 17th
  century in Antwerp: the Firm
  Forchoudt', *Historical Sources for the
  Study of Flemish Art*, vol. I, Antwerp,
  1931.
Devonshire, 6th Duke of, *Handbook to
  Chatsworth and Hardwick*, Privately
  Printed, 1845.
Digby, George Wingfield, *Elizabethan
  Embroidery*, Faber & Faber, 1963.
Digby, George Wingfield, *The Tapestry
  Collection. Medieval and Renaissance*,
  Victoria & Albert Museum, 1980.

Durant, David, *Bess of Hardwick*,
  Weidenfeld & Nicolson, 1977.
Durant, David, *Arbella Stuart*,
  Weidenfeld & Nicolson, 1978.
Durant, David, and Riden, Philip,
  (eds.), *The Building of Hardwick Hall*,
  (2 parts) Derbyshire Record Society,
  vols. IV, 1980, and IX, 1984.
Ellis, Henry, *Original Letters*, 2nd
  Series (4 vols.), 1827; 3rd series
  (4 vols), 1846.
Gage, John, *The History and Antiquities
  of Hengrave in Suffolk*, 1822.
Gilbert, Christopher; Lomax, James;
  Wells-Cole, Anthony, *Country House
  Floors, 1660-1850*, Exhibition
  Catalogue, Temple Newsam House,
  Leeds City Art Galleries, 1987.
Girouard, Mark, *Life in the English
  Country House*, Yale University Press,
  1978.
Girouard, Mark, *Robert Smythson and
  the Elizabethan County House*, Yale
  University Press, 1983.
Girouard, Mark, 'Elizabethan
  Chatsworth', *Country Life*,
  22 November, 1973.
Girouard, Mark, *Guide to Hardwick
  Hall*, National Trust, 1972 and 1989.
Halliwell, James Orchard, *Ancient
  Inventories … of the Sixteenth and
  Seventeenth Centuries*, Privately
  Printed, 1854.
Handover, P. M., *Arbella Stuart*, Eyre
  & Spottiswoode, 1957.
Hunter, Joseph, *The History of
  Hallamshire*, enlarged edition by
  Alfred Gatty, Sheffield, 1869.
Hunter, Joseph, 'An Acount of the
  Expenses of the two Brothers,
  Mr. Henry and Mr. William
  Cavendish, … at Eton College,
  beginning October 21st, 2nd
  Elizabeth, 1560', *The Retrospective
  Review*, 2nd Series, vol. II, 1828.
Hunter, Joseph, 'Biographical
  Memories of Sir William St. Loe',
  The Retrospective Review, 2nd Series,
  vol. II, 1828.
'An Inventory of all the Household
  Goods and Furniture belonging to
  George Earl of Shrewsbury at
  Sheffield-Castle and the Lodge, 1582',
  British Archaeological Journal, vol. 30,
  1874.
Jourdain, Margaret, *The History of
  English Secular Embroidery*, Kegan
  Paul, 1910.
Jourdain, Margaret, 'Needlework
  at Hardwick', *Country Life*,
  26 February, 1927.
Jourdain, Margaret, 'Some Tapestries
  at Hardwick Hall', *Country Life*,
  26 March, 1927.
Jourdain, Margaret, 'Sixteenth
  Century Embroidery with
  Emblems', *The Burlington Magazine*,
  vol. XI, 1907.

Kendrick, A. F., *English Needlework*,
  2nd revised edition, A. & C. Black,
  1967.
Kennett, Bishop White, *Memoirs of the
  Family of Cavendish*, 1708.
King, Donald, and Sylvester, David,
  *The Eastern Carpet in the Western
  World from the 15th to the 17th Century*,
  Arts Council Exhibition Catalogue,
  1983.
Kingsford, C. L., 'The Inventory of
  Leicester House', *Archaeolgia*,
  vol. 73, 1922-3.
Leader, J. D., *Mary Queen of Scots in
  Captivity*, Sheffield, 1880.
Lees-Milne, James, *The Bachelor Duke:
  A Life of William Spencer Cavendish,
  6th Duke of Devonshire, 1790-1858*,
  John Murray, 1991.
Leverson-Gower, the Hon. F., *Letters
  of Harriet Countess Granville,
  1810-1845*, 1894.
Leverson-Gower, G. L., *Harry-O;
  Letters of Lady Harriet Cavendish,
  1796-1809*, 1940.
Levey, Santina M., 'The Broderers'
  Work', in *The Inventory of King Henry
  VIII*, ed. David Starkey,
  Antiquaries Society of London/
  Harvey Miller Publishers, 1998/9.
Lodge, Edmund, *Illustrations of British
  History, Biography, and Manners, in the
  Reigns of Henry VIII, etc.*, 2nd
  revised edition (3 vols.), 1838.
Mitchell, David, 'Linen Diaper and
  Damask', in *The Inventory of King
  Henry VIII*, ed. David Starkey,
  Antiquaries Society of London/
  Harvey Miller Publishers, 1998/9.
Montgomery, Florence, *Textiles in
  America, 1650-1870*, W. W. Norton
  & Co., 1984.
Nevinson, John L., 'An Elizabethan
  Herbarium: Embroideries by Bess of
  Hardwick after the Woodcuts of
  Mattioli', *National Trust Year Book*,
  1975-6.
Nevinson, John L., 'Embroidered by
  Queen and Countess', *Country Life*,
  22 January, 1976.
Nevinson, John L., 'English Domestic
  Embroidery Patterns of the 16th and
  17th centuries', *Walpole Society*,
  vol. XXVIII, 1939-40.
Nevinson, John L., 'Stitched for Bess
  of Hardwick. Embroideries at
  Hardwick Hall, Derbyshire', *Country
  Life*, 29 November, 1973.
Nichols, John, *The Progresses and Public
  Processions of Queen Elizabeth*, 2nd
  edition (3 vols), 1823.
Pearson, John, *Stags & Serpents: The
  Story of the House of Cavendish and the
  Dukes of Devonshire*, Macmillan, 1983.
Pomfret, Thomas, *The Life of the Right
  Honourable And Religious Lady
  Christian, Late Countess Dowager of
  Devonshire*, 1685.

Roethlisberger, Marcel, 'The Ulysses Tapestries at Hardwick Hall', *Gazette des Beaux-Arts*, 6th Series, vol. 77, 1972.

Stallybrass, Basil, 'Bess of Hardwick's Buildings and Building Accounts', *Archaeologia*, vol. 64, 1913.

Starkey, David (ed.), *The Inventory of King Henry VIII*, (3 vols.) Antiquaries Society of London/ Harvey Miller Publishers, 1998/9.

Steen, S. J., *The Letters of Lady Arbella Stuart*, Oxford University Press, 1994.

Stone, Lawrence, *The Crisis of the Aristocracy, 1558–1641*, Oxford University Press, 1965.

Stone, L., and Stone, J.C.F., *An Open Elite?* Oxford University Press, 1984.

Strickland, Agnes, *The Letters of Mary Queen of Scots*, (2 vols.) 1844.

Swain, Margaret, *Historical Needlework*, Barrie & Jenkins, 1970.

Swain, Margaret, *The Needlework of Mary Queen of Scots*, Van Nostrand Reinhold Co., 1973.

Thompson, Francis, *A History of Chatsworth*, 1949.

Thomson, Thomas, *Collection of Inventories and Other records of the Royal Wardrobe & Jewelhouse*, Edinburgh, 1815.

Thornton, Peter, *Seventeenth Century Interior Decoration in England, France & Holland*, Yale University Press/Paul Mellon Centre for Studies in British Art, 1983.

Thornton, Peter, *The Italian Renaissance Interior, 1400–1600*, Weidenfeld & Nicolson, 1991.

Torrington, 5th Viscount, *The Torrington Diaries Containing the Tours through England and Wales of the Hon. John Byng (Later 5th Viscount Torrington) between the Years 1781 & 1794*, (4 vols.) ed. C. Bruyn Andrews, Eyre & Spottiswoode, 1938.

Unwin, George, *The Guilds and Companies of London*, 1908.

Walpole, Horace, *Walpole's Journals of Visits to Country Seats*, ed. Mrs Paget Toynbee, *Walpole Society*, vol. XVI, 1927–9.

Walpole, Horace, *The Letters of Horace Walpole*, ed. Mrs Paget Toynbee, Clarendon Press, vol. IV, 1904.

Waterer, John, *Spanish Leather*, 1971.

Wells-Cole, Anthony, *Art and Decoration in Elizabethan and Jacobean England: The Influence of Continental Prints, 1558–1625*, Yale University Press/Paul Mellon Centre for Studies in British Art, 1997.

Williams, E. Carleton, *Bess of Hardwick*, Longmans, Green & Co., 1959.

Wood, A.C., (ed.), 'Fox's "Mr Harrie Cavendish: His journey to and from Constantinople, 1589"', *Camden Miscellany*, 3rd series, vol. 64.

Monetary and other values

It is impossible to convert sixteenth century costs into present day money, or to value in modern terms the land, houses and goods that made up the wealth of well-to-do Elizabethans. Labour costs were low but some raw materials and manufactured goods were expensive and, as in the case of the New Hall at Hardwick, it was possible for a building to be worth less than its contents, of which textiles formed a major part. They varied in quality but the finest were very expensive – on a par with gold and silver plate.

England's export trade was dominated by raw wool and woollen cloths but the steady increase in disposable personal wealth was drawing in a growing quantity of luxury textiles from Europe, the Near East and increasingly from India and China. Such goods were valued for their rarity and beauty, not simply for their high cost, and they were carefully preserved for future generations.

Money, numerals and measurements

The Hardwick accounts are recorded almost entirely in pounds, shillings and pence, although coins of other denominations did exist. The pound sign [£, li or l] reflected its Latin origins as a pound weight of silver [libra] and the sign for a penny was still d for denarius, a Roman coin.

There were twenty shillings to the pound, and twelve pennies to the shilling; that is, 144 pennies to the pound. The penny was also divided into half- and quarter-pence. Because the purchasing power of shillings and pennies was considerably greater than today, they were often used alone, even when the total went above twenty shillings.

Roman rather than Arabic numerals were used in the account books until the end of the sixteenth century: i, ij, iij, iv, v, vj, vij, viij, ix, x [1 to 10], xj [11], xx [20], l [50], c or C [100], m or M [1,000]. Multiples of twenty (a score) were sometimes used when quantities were written out in words rather than numerals.

The standard measurement for English cloth was a yard of 36 inches (914 cm). An older measurement, called an ell, was used for imported cloth. Its length varied from country to country (the English ell was 45 inches) but the only one used in the accounts is the Flemish ell of 27 inches (roughly three-quarters of a yard) by which the tapestries, fine linens and linen damask from Flanders were sold.

Threads, braids and laces made of silk and metal threads were sold by weight, usually by the ounce [oz] and occasionally by the pound [lb]. There were sixteen ounces in a pound, which was equivalent to 0·453 kilograms.

Dates

Two methods of recording the year were used. One was according to the old Julian Calendar in which the year began on 25 March; this is the calendar used in the text with the period between 1 January and 24 March given two year dates, e.g. 1601/2. The other was the regnal year, which was calculated from 17 November 1558, when Queen Elizabeth had come to the throne. Bess thus recorded a gift of £20 to 'my sonne William at new yeares tyde in the xlj[st] [41st] year of her myt[s] reagn', i.e. in January 1598/9.

GLOSSARY

Aglet/aiglet: a metal tag at the end of a lace, originally plain but also made of gold or silver and ornamented with precious stones, enamels, etc.

Anticks/antiques: Renaissance pattern structures and fanciful images based on decorations found in the ruins of ancient (or antique) Rome.

Arras: a term initially used in England to denote only the finest tapestry, particularly that incorporating gold and silver thread. By the late sixteenth century it was applied indiscriminately to any tapestry.

Baize: a heavy woollen cloth, usually raised or napped and felted to provide a smooth surface. Used to cover billiard tables.

Bays/bayes: a napped fabric with a worsted warp and a woollen weft.

Billament: a decorated band, often set with jewels, applied to the stiffened head-dress, known as a French hood, worn by women in the mid-sixteenth century.

Billets: a heraldic motif of an upright rectangle said to represent either a short length of wood or a gold bar.

Buckerom/buckram: a coarse cloth made of hemp, stiffened with gum or starch.

Changeable taffeta: a plain weave silk with warp and weft of different colours; the dominant colour varies according to the play of light.

Chintz: Indian painted and printed cotton of the sixteenth–eighteenth centuries. The term was also applied to European copies of the late seventeenth and eighteenth centuries.

Cloth of gold/silver: a silk fabric with an additional weft of metal thread secured by a near-invisible binding warp. Plain cloth of gold had a yellow base and cloth of silver a white one, but other colours were used to make 'purple cloth of gold', etc. See also tinsel and tissue.

Confidente: a mid-eighteenth century French term for a sofa with ends that curved inwards so the occupants almost faced one another.

Cope: a ceremonial cloak worn by the participants on important ecclesiastical occasions.

Crane-coloured: ash-grey.

Damask: a fabric in which a reversible pattern is formed by the contrasting sides (or faces) of the weave – normally, but not always, satin. The warp is usually finer and more closely packed than the weft so the pattern, formed by the weft, appears duller and rougher than the shiny warp. Damasks of silk, linen and wool were woven,

both with complex figurative designs and simple geometric patterns. See also diaper.

Diaper: a damask weave, in either satin or twill, with a small, all-over lattice or diamond pattern. In the early sixteenth century, the term was applied to all patterned linens and in 1551 Bess was still describing her table linen with the *Story of Abraham* as 'fyne dyaper.'

Double cloth: a fabric woven with two warps, one above the other. It can be made with two separate wefts or with a single weft taken through each warp in turn. The two layers can be linked by 'ties' within the weave or joined down one or both selvages (edges).

Double shaft: a shaft is a group of heddle bars, which control the lowering or raising of warp threads. An increase in the number of shafts, makes the weaving of more complex structures and patterns possible.

Ell/elne/nell: a unit of length used in many parts of Europe, although, by the late sixteenth century, it was being replaced in England by the yard. The length of the ell varied from country to country; in England it was 45 inches (114 cm) and in Flanders, 27 inches (68·5 cm).

En suite: a matching set, for example, of furniture.

Entablature: term in classical architecture indicating the parts supported by the columns.

Felted wool: the fabric is napped, sheared and shrunk by a process known as fulling, so the weave structure is no longer visible.

Festoon curtains: a decorative effect achieved by threading cords through rings sewn in vertical rows on the backs of curtains. When pulled up, the curtains bunched into swags at the top of the window.

Forrest work: an alternative term for large-leafed verdures, often incorporating animals, or hunting and other woodland activities.

Fret/frettes, fretwork: pattern of intersecting vertical and horizontal lines.

Grotesques: a name derived from the Italian *grotte*, for the underground ruins of ancient Rome. Another name for anticks/antiques.

Haraton/harateen: a worsted furnishing fabric with a plain weave sometimes watered or crushed between patterned rollers to produce a waved effect in the surface.

Harden: a coarse fabric made from hemp (thick, strong fibres from a

herbaceous plant) or tow (broken or poor quality flax).

Herm: a three-quarter-length figure (male or female) rising from a pedestal.

Huckaback: a double-sided linen fabric with geometric patterns formed by loose floats of warp and weft threads, which made the cloth more absorbent; it was used for towels.

Inlay/intarsia: a means of producing a decorative effect by inserting pieces of differently coloured woods or ivory into a solid wooden base. See also Markentrie/marquetry.

Japanned/japanning: a European copy of oriental lacquer.

Knots: an English name for a formal interlace, as in a knot garden.

Laid work: a method of covering a ground fabric with close parallel lines of thread, held only by tiny stitches at each end. Large areas are usually further secured by laying a contrasting thread in an open pattern on top and couching (holding) it down with a third thread.

Litter: a substantial covered chair carried on men's shoulders or slung on poles between two horses.

Markentrie/marquetry: now used only of decorative patterns built-up with pieces of veneer applied to the surface of an object. In the 1601 inventories it is used to describe inlay.

Murrey-coloured: a purplish-red, similar to a ripe mulberry.

Mercer: a dealer in silk, as opposed to a woollen or linen draper.

Nap/napped: a cloth finishing technique whereby the fibres on the surface of a woollen cloth are brushed or raised to form a short pile.

Nel: see ell.

Ogee: a curving line composed of joined S-shapes.

Orphrey: decorated bands applied to ecclesiastical vestments.

Passementerie: a French term for trimmings – fringes, tassels, braids, toggles, etc.

Perle: pearl. See also purl.

Petepoynt/*petit point*: the French name for tent or half-cross stitch.

Plush: a plain woollen velvet used in the eighteenth century for men's clothing and increasingly for furnishings. By the mid-nineteenth century it sometimes had a stamped or impressed pattern.

Pole-screen: a small fireside screen consisting of an upright pole with either an adjustable shield-shaped screen or a cross-pole from which a textile panel was hung like a banner.

Purl: a form of metal embroidery thread coiled like a tiny spring.

Satin weave: a binding system which produces a shiny surface by floating the warp threads over four or sometimes seven threads before they are bound; the binding points are staggered making them virtually invisible.

Say/saye: a light-weight twilled woollen cloth, in the seventeenth century sometimes woven with a silk warp, sized to give it a sheen.

Silvines: flowers, possibly silverwort.

Spandrel: a triangular shape formed between the upper curve of an arch and the entablature.

Sparver: a bed without posts but with a roof or tester suspended from the ceiling of the room. The Best Bed at the New Hall was of this type, although by 1600, it was no longer fashionable.

Statute lace: a type of braid. The origins of the name are obscure but suggest that its manufacture or use had once been controlled by statute.

Strapwork: a Renaissance device for controlling a design with interlaced bands resembling leather straps. In northern Europe the straps were often drawn as metal bars.

Sweet-bag: a small bag containing sweet-smelling herbs.

Tabby weave: alternative name for plain weave in which the warp and weft threads interlace in a simple over-one-under-one sequence.

Tinsel: in the sixteenth century, a valuable type of cloth of gold or silver elaborated with flat metal strip.

Tissue: in the sixteenth century, the most expensive form of cloth of gold or silver decorated with raised loops of metal threads. It was also woven with a velvet ground.

Twill: a weave in which two or more warp threads pass (or float) over two or more weft threads, and the binding points are offset on each successive row to form marked diagonal lines.

Vallans/double vallans: valances or pelmets hung round the top of a bed to cover the rods and rings on which the bed-curtains were suspended. On grand beds, a second set was fitted to cover the inner side of the rods. Base valances (pants) were hung at mattress level to fill the space below the bed.

Verdures: tapestries patterned with small flowers, leaves and sometimes birds and animals. In the late sixteenth century, exceptionally large-leafed foliage was fashionable combined with animals and sometimes figures.

Watchett-coloured: a light blue.

INDEX